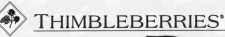 THIMBLEBERRIES®

Beautiful Blocks
for Beautiful Quilts

Landauer Publishing, LLC

THIMBLEBERRIES®
Beautiful Blocks
for Beautiful Quilts

by Lynette Jensen

Copyright © 2012 by Landauer Publishing, LLC
Projects Copyright© 2012 by Lynette Jensen

This book was designed, produced, and published by Landauer Publishing, LLC
3100 101st Street, Urbandale, IA 50322
800-557-2144; 515-287-2144; www.landauerpub.com

President/Publisher: Jeramy Lanigan Landauer
Vice President of Sales and Administration: Kitty Jacobson
Editor: Jeri Simon
Art Director: Laurel Albright
Creative Director: Lynette Jensen
Photographer: Sue Voegtlin
Technical Writer: Sue Bahr
Technical Illustrator: Lisa Kirchoff

We also wish to thank the support staff of the Thimbleberries® Design Studio:
Sherry Husske, Julie Jergens, Virginia Brodd, Ardelle Paulson, and machine quilters:
Clarine Howe and Connie Albin.

The following manufacturers are licensed to sell Thimbleberries® products:
Thimbleberries® Rugs (www.colonialmills.com);
Thimbleberries® Quilt Stencils (www.quiltingcreations.com);
Thimbleberries® Sewing Thread (www.robison-anton.com and www.Sulky.com); and
Thimbleberries® Fabrics (RJR Fabrics available at independent quilt shops).

This book is printed on acid-free paper.

Printed in United States 10 9 8 7 6 5 4 3 2 1

Library of Congress Control Number: 2012937348

ISBN 13: 978-1-935726-24-1

About
Lynette Jensen

Lynette Jensen is recognized as a leading fabric and pattern designer in the independent quilt industry, a best-selling author of dozens of books with nearly a million copies sold, and a foremost educator and authority on the subjects of quilting and decorating.

As the founder and president of Thimbleberries®, Lynette has been at the forefront of the home arts industry. Thimbleberries® unique offering of coordinated fabric collections and detailed project patterns offer consumers the ability to put them together in a clear, graphic sense to create a quilted product they can enjoy making and be proud to display.

Another successful component in the Thimbleberries® brand mix is the Thimbleberries® Club program which reaches quilters around the world.

Designing from her traditional point of view, Lynette introduces numerous all-cotton fabric collections every year. In addition to fabric, patterns, and books, other products carrying the Thimbleberries® name and signature look include embroidery designs, stencils, and thread.

Lynette Jensen

Contents

Basket Sampler Throw
14

Blocks 1-8 19

Quilt Center Assembly & Putting It All Together . . . 29

Basket Sampler Queen 33

Contents

Apple Basket Wall Quilt **36**

April Showers Table Runner **40**

Heart Basket Table Runner **44**

Pine Tree Basket Wall Quilt **48**

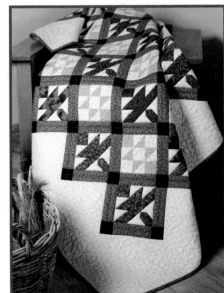

Winter Spruce Quilt **54**

Contents

Sunrise Throw
60

Blocks 1-6 62

Quilt Center Assembly & Putting It All Together . . . 71

Contents

Wedding Quilt 74

Spring Fling
Throw 80

Summer Surprise
Quilt 84

Contents

Calendar Sampler Throw
88

Blocks 1-12 90

Quilt Center Assembly & Putting It All Together . . 111

Contents

Apple Stand Table Runner ... 114

Potholders ... 116
House Potholder
Star Potholder
Pumpkin Potholder
Tree Potholder

City Tote ... 124

General Instructions & Glossary 130

Introduction

Years ago, I created Thimbleberries® Block-of-the-Month program as a way to enable quilters with limited time to create quilts of enduring beauty. Quilters worldwide embraced the concept. Today, Thimbleberries Block-of-the-Month programs are a staple in the quilting industry. Thousands of quilters take part in Thimbleberries® Clubs that meet monthly in independent quilt shops.

In this book, I've assembled some of my most popular traditional pieced block motifs and present them in a variety of color options and patterns to provide you with choices for creating a myriad of beautiful quilt projects for your home.

From collection to collection, from season to season and from year to year you can create with confidence knowing that the Thimbleberries color palette will always blend beautifully and will stand the test of time.

To help you successfully complete your quilts, my staff and I have worked hard to create a system of quilt-making that uses clear and simple instructions you can rely on. Even first-time quilters can build confidence and skills.

Whichever project you choose—a bed quilt, table runner or wall quilt—enjoy the journey of creating beautiful quilted keepsakes that welcome family and friends to a warm and inviting home.

Basket Sampler
Block 1

Basket Sampler
Block 2

Basket Sampler
Block 3

Basket Sampler
Block 4

Basket Sampler
Block 5

Basket Sampler
Block 6

Basket Sampler
Block 7

Basket Sampler
Block 8

Sunrise
Block 1

Sunrise
Block 2

Sunrise
Block 3

Sunrise
Block 4

Sunrise
Block 5

Sunrise
Block 6

Calendar Sampler
January Block

Calendar Sampler
February Block

Calendar Sampler
March Block

Calendar Sampler
April Block

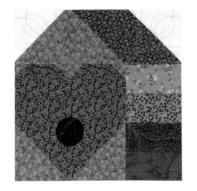

Calendar Sampler
May Block

Calendar Sampler
June Block

Calendar Sampler
July Block

Calendar Sampler
August Block

Calendar Sampler
September Block

Calendar Sampler
October Block

Calendar Sampler
November Block

Calendar Sampler
December Block

Basket Sampler

Hearts and flowers, apples and pine trees
fill Thimbleberries® baskets with design blocks
you can use in a myriad of creative ways.

Whether you choose to stitch the 8-block
Basket Sampler Throw or begin with a
single block inspiration, as in the seasonal
Pine Tree Basket Wall Quilt, you will enjoy the ease,
satisfaction and beauty that is Thimbleberries®.

Basket Sampler Throw

68 x 74-inches

Fabrics & Supplies

1-3/4 yards **RED PRINT** for blocks, block 6 leaf appliqués, top section, bottom section flower appliqués, spacers, middle border

2-1/8 yards **BEIGE PRINT** for background

7/8 yard **GREEN PRINT #1** for blocks, block 2 leaf appliqués, bottom section

3/8 yard **GOLD PRINT** for blocks, block 1 heart appliqués, bottom section flower center appliqués

1/2 yard **BLUE PRINT #1** for block 3, checkerboard

1/4 yard **BLUE PRINT #2** for flying geese

3/8 yard **BROWN PRINT** for blocks

2 yards **BLUE PRINT #3** for block 7, inner border, outer border

1/2 yard **GREEN PRINT #2** for spacer rectangles

2/3 yard **RED DIAGONAL PRINT** for binding

4-1/8 yards for backing

quilt batting, at least 74 x 80-inches

paper-backed fusible web

tear-away fabric stabilizer (optional)

matching thread for appliqué

Before beginning this project, read through **Getting Started** *on page 131.*

Top Section

Cutting

From **RED PRINT**:
- Cut 1, 2-7/8 x 44-inch strip
- Cut 1, 2-1/2 x 44-inch strip. From strip cut: 16, 2-1/2-inch squares

From **BEIGE PRINT**:
- Cut 1, 2-7/8 x 44-inch strip
- Cut 2, 2-1/2 x 44-inch strips. From strips cut: 32, 2-1/2-inch squares

Piecing

Note: *Refer to arrows on diagrams for pressing.*

Step 1   With right sides together, layer the 2-7/8 x 44-inch **RED** and **BEIGE** strips. Press together, but do not sew. Cut the layered strip into squares. Cut the layered squares in half diagonally to make 24 sets of triangles. Stitch 1/4-inch from the diagonal edge of each pair of triangles; press.

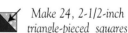

Crosscut 12, 2-7/8-inch squares

Make 24, 2-1/2-inch triangle-pieced squares

Step 2   Referring to diagram, lay out (3) triangle-pieced squares, (2) 2-1/2-inch **RED** squares, and (4) 2-1/2-inch **BEIGE** squares. Sew squares into rows; press. Sew rows together; press. <u>At this point each block should measure 6-1/2-inches square.</u>

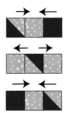

Make 8 blocks

Step 3   Referring to diagram, sew the Step 2 blocks together end-to-end; press. <u>At this point the top section should measure 6-1/2 x 48-1/2-inches.</u>

Top Section

Bottom Section

Cutting

From **BEIGE** and **GREEN PRINT #1**:
- Cut 1, 6-7/8 x 44-inch strip from *each* fabric.
  From **EACH** strip cut:
  4, 6-7/8-inch squares. Cut the squares in half diagonally to make 8 triangles from each fabric.

6-7/8-inch square   *6-7/8-inch square*

Piecing

Note: *Refer to arrows on diagrams for pressing.*

Step 1   Trace (8) flowers and flower centers on page 31 on the paper side of the fusible web leaving a small margin between each shape. Cut shapes apart.

Note: *Refer to **Paper-Backed Fusible Web Appliqué** on page 30 for complete instructions for appliquéing.*

Step 2   Place flowers and flower centers on **BEIGE** triangles; fuse in place and zigzag stitch using matching thread. Sew together appliquéd triangles and **GREEN #1** triangles in pairs; press.

↗ *bias edge*
Make 8

Make 8,
6-1/2-inch blocks

Step 3   Sew together 4 blocks; press. Make 2 units. Sew units together; press. <u>At this point the bottom section should measure 6-1/2 x 48-1/2-inches.</u>

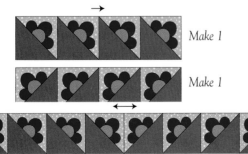

Make 1

Make 1

Bottom Section

Vertical Lattice Sections

Cutting

From **BLUE PRINT #1**:
- Cut 3, 2-1/2 x 44-inch strips

From **BLUE PRINT #2**:
- Cut 2, 2-1/2 x 44-inch strips. From strips cut:
  18, 2-1/2 x 4-1/2-inch rectangles

From **BEIGE PRINT**:
- Cut 4, 2-1/2 x 44-inch strips. From strips cut:
  18, 2-1/2 x 4-1/2-inch rectangles
  18, 2-1/2-inch squares
- Cut 3 more 2-1/2 x 44-inch strips

From **RED PRINT**:
- Cut 2, 6-1/2-inch squares

Checkerboard Section Piecing

Note: *Refer to arrows on diagrams for pressing.*

Step 1   Aligning long edges, sew 2-1/2 x 44-inch **BLUE #1** strips to both side edges of a 2-1/2 x 44-inch **BEIGE** strip. Press seam allowances toward **BLUE #1** strips referring to *Hints and Helps for Pressing Strip Sets* on page 138. Cut strip set into segments.

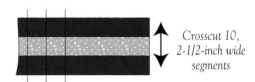

Crosscut 10, 2-1/2-inch wide segments

Step 2   Aligning long edges, sew 2-1/2 x 44-inch **BEIGE** strips to both side edges of a 2-1/2 x 44-inch **BLUE #1** strip; press. Cut strip set into segments.

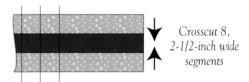

Crosscut 8, 2-1/2-inch wide segments

Step 3   To make each checkerboard section sew together (5) Step 1 segments and (4) Step 2 segments; press. <u>At this point each checkerboard section should measure 6-1/2 x 18-1/2-inches.</u>

Make 2

Flying Geese Section Piecing

Note: *Refer to arrows on diagrams for pressing.*

Step 1   With right sides together, position a
2-1/2 x 4-1/2-inch **BEIGE** rectangle on the left
corner of a 2-1/2 x 4-1/2-inch **BLUE #2** rectangle.
Draw a diagonal line on the **BEIGE** rectangle;
stitch on the line. Trim seam allowance to 1/4-inch;
press. Repeat this process at the right corner of the
BLUE #2 rectangle using a 2-1/2-inch **BEIGE**
square. At this point each flying geese unit should
measure 2-1/2 x 6-1/2-inches.

Make 10

Step 2   With right sides together, position a 2-1/2-inch
BEIGE square on the left corner of a
2-1/2 x 4-1/2-inch **BLUE #2** rectangle. Draw a
diagonal line on the square; stitch on the line.
Trim seam allowance to 1/4-inch; press. Repeat this
process at the right corner of the **BLUE #2**
rectangle using a 2-1/2 x 4-1/2-inch **BEIGE**
rectangle. At this point each flying geese unit
should measure 2-1/2 x 6-1/2-inches.

Make 8

Step 3   Sew together (5) Step 1 units
and (4) Step 2 units; press.
At this point each flying
geese section should measure
6-1/2 x 18-1/2-inches.

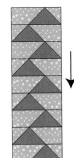

Make 2

Step 4   Sew together a flying geese section, a checkerboard
section, and a 6-1/2-inch **RED** square; press.
At this point each vertical lattice section should
measure 6-1/2 x 42-1/2-inches.

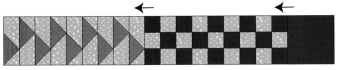

Make 2 Vertical Lattice Sections

Quilt Center Basket Blocks

Makes 8 basket blocks

Cutting

Note: *Label the pieces for each block. Keep the pieces for each block in a separate plastic bag to avoid confusion.*

From **GREEN PRINT #1**:
- Cut 1, 4-1/2 x 44-inch strip for **block #1**.
  From strip cut:
  2, 4-1/2-inch squares
  1, 2-7/8-inch square
  4, 2-1/2-inch squares

- Cut 1, 2-1/2 x 44-inch strip for **block #3**.
  From strip cut:
  1, 2-1/2 x 12-1/2-inch rectangle
  2, 2-1/2 x 4-1/2-inch rectangles

- Cut 1, 2-7/8 x 44-inch strip for **block #4**.
  From strip cut:
  1, 2-7/8-inch square
  1, 2-1/2 x 6-1/2-inch rectangle
  1, 2-1/2 x 4-1/2-inch rectangle
  2, 2-1/2-inch squares

- Cut 1, 7-inch square for **block #6**.
  Cut the square diagonally into quarters
  to make 4 triangles. You will be using
  only 3 triangles.

- Cut 1, 4-1/2-inch square and
  1, 2 x 21-inch *bias* strip for handle

7-inch square

From **BEIGE PRINT**:
- Cut 1, 6-1/2 x 44-inch strip for **block #1**.
  From strip cut:
  2, 6-1/2-inch squares
  1, 4-1/2 x 6-1/2-inch rectangle
  1, 2-7/8-inch square
  4, 2-1/2 x 4-1/2-inch rectangles
  2, 2-1/2-inch squares

- Cut 1, 12-7/8-inch square. Cut the
  square in half diagonally to make 2
  triangles. You will be using 1 triangle
  for **block #2** and 1 for **block #5**.

- Cut 1, 6-1/2 x 44-inch strip for
  block #3. From strip cut:
  2, 6-1/2-inch squares
  2, 4-1/2-inch squares
  4, 2-1/2-inch squares

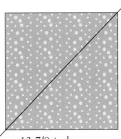

12-7/8-inch square

- Cut 1, 6-5/8 x 44-inch strip for **block #4**.
  From strip cut:
  1, 6-5/8-inch square
  1, 2-7/8-inch square
  2, 2-5/8 x 8-5/8-inch rectangles
  2, 2-5/8 x 12-7/8-inch rectangles
  4, 2-1/2-inch squares
  2, 1-1/2-inch squares

Note: The block #4 pieces will also be used to make the block #7 handle.

- Cut 1, 2-1/2 x 44-inch strip for **block #5**.
  From strip cut:
  1, 2-1/2 x 4-1/2-inch rectangle
  3, 2-1/2-inch squares

Note: The 12-7/8-inch triangle was cut with block #2.

- Cut 1, 12-7/8-inch square for **block #6**. Cut the square in half diagonally to make 2 triangles. You will be using only 1 triangle.

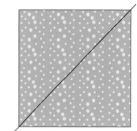
12-7/8-inch square

- Cut 1, 6-7/8 x 44-inch strip for **block #8**.
  From strip cut:
  1, 6-7/8-inch square
  2, 6-1/2-inch squares
  2, 5-1/2-inch squares

From **RED PRINT:**
  Refer to cutting diagram.

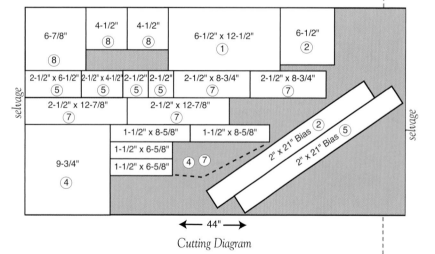
Cutting Diagram

- Cut 1, 6-7/8 x 44-inch strip. From strip cut:
  1, 6-7/8-inch square for **block #8**
  2, 4-1/2-inch squares for **block #8**
  1, 6-1/2 x 12-1/2-inch rectangle for **block #1**
  1, 6-1/2-inch square for **block #2**

- Cut 1, 2-1/2 x 44-inch strip. From strip cut:
  1, 2-1/2 x 6-1/2-inch rectangle for **block #5**
  1, 2-1/2 x 4-1/2-inch rectangle for **block #5**
  2, 2-1/2-inch squares for **block #5**
  2, 2-1/2 x 8-3/4-inch rectangles for **block #7**

- Cut 1, 2-1/2 x <u>28-inch</u> strip. From strip cut:
  2, 2-1/2 x 12-7/8-inch rectangles for **block #7**

- Cut 1, 9-3/4-inch square for **block #4**. Cut the square diagonally into quarters to make 4 triangles. You will be using only 2 triangles.

9-3/4-inch square

- Cut 2, 1-1/2 x 8-5/8-inch rectangles for **blocks #4/#7**

- Cut 2, 1-1/2 x 6-5/8-inch rectangles for **blocks #4/#7**

- Cut 2, 2 x 21-inch **bias** strips for **blocks #2/#5**

From **BROWN PRINT:**
- Cut 1, 9-3/4 x 44-inch strip for **block #2**. From strip cut:
  1, 9-3/4-inch square. Cut the square diagonally into quarters to make 4 triangles. You will be using only 2 triangles for apple basket.

9-3/4-inch square

- Cut 4, 2-1/2-inch squares
- Cut 2, 4-1/2-inch squares for **block #6**
- Cut 1, 6-1/2 x 12-1/2-inch rectangle for **block #8**

From **BLUE PRINT #1:**
- Cut 1, 6-1/2 x 44-inch strip for **block #3**.
  From strip cut:
  1, 6-1/2 x 12-1/2-inch rectangle
  2, 4-1/2-inch squares

From **GOLD PRINT:**
- Cut 1, 9-3/4 x 44-inch strip for **block #5**.
  From strip cut:
  1, 9-3/4-inch square.
  Cut the square diagonally into quarters to make 4 triangles. You will be using only 2 triangles.

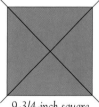
9-3/4-inch square

- Cut 1, 2-1/2-inch square
- Cut 1, 4-5/8-inch square for **block #7**

From **BLUE PRINT #3:**
- Cut 1, 2-5/8 x 44-inch strip for **block #7**.
  From strip cut: 2, 2-5/8 x 8-3/4-inch rectangle
  2, 2-5/8 x 4-5/8-inch rectangles

Basket Block #1 Piecing

Note: *Refer to arrows on diagrams for pressing.*

Step 1   With right sides together, position a 2-1/2-inch **GREEN #1** square on the upper left corner of a 4-1/2 x 6-1/2-inch **BEIGE** rectangle. Draw a diagonal line on the square; stitch on the line. Trim seam allowance to 1/4-inch; press. Repeat this process at the upper right corner of the rectangle.

Make 1

Step 2   With right sides together, position a 2-1/2-inch **GREEN #1** square on the corner of a 2-1/2 x 4-1/2-inch **BEIGE** rectangle. Draw a diagonal line on the square; stitch on the line, trim, and press. Repeat this process reversing the direction of the stitching line. Sew a 2-1/2-inch **BEIGE** square to the top edge of each of the units; press. Sew the units to both side edges of the Step 1 unit; press. <u>At this point the unit should measure 6-1/2 x 8-1/2-inches.</u>

   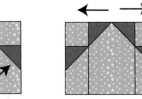

Make 1   *Make 1*   *Make 1 unit*

Step 3   With right sides together, layer the 2-7/8-inch **GREEN #1** and **BEIGE** squares. Press together, but do not sew. Cut the layered square in half diagonally to make 2 sets of triangles. Stitch 1/4-inch from the diagonal edge of each pair of triangles; press. Sew a 2-1/2 x 4-1/2-inch **BEIGE** rectangle to the top edge of each triangle-pieced square. <u>At this point each unit should measure 2-1/2 x 6-1/2-inches.</u>

Make 2, 2-1/2-inch triangle-pieced squares   *Make 1*   *Make 1*

Step 4   Sew the Step 3 units to both side edges of the Step 2 unit; press. <u>At this point the basket handle unit should measure 6-1/2 x 12-1/2-inches.</u> Staystitch around the unit to secure the seams before adding the appliqué.

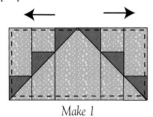

Make 1

Step 5   Make a template using the heart shape on page 31. Trace (3) hearts on the paper side of the fusible web leaving a small margin between each shape. Cut shapes apart.

Note: *Refer to **Paper-Backed Fusible Web Appliqué** on page 30 for complete instructions for appliquéing.*

Step 6   Place hearts on basket handle unit; fuse in place and zigzag stitch using matching thread.

Make 1

Step 7 With right sides together, position a 4-1/2-inch **GREEN #1** square on the corner of a 6-1/2-inch **BEIGE** square. Draw a diagonal line on the small square; stitch on the line, trim, and press.

Make 2

Step 8 With right sides together, position a Step 5 unit on the corner of the 6-1/2 x 12-1/2-inch **RED** rectangle. Draw a diagonal line on the pieced unit; stitch on the line, trim, and press.

Repeat this process at the opposite corner of the rectangle. <u>At this point the basket base should measure 6-1/2 x 12-1/2-inches.</u>

Make 1

Step 9 Sew handle and base units together; press. <u>At this point the basket block should measure 12-1/2-inches square.</u>

Make 1

Basket Block #2 Piecing

Note: *Refer to arrows on diagrams for pressing.*

Step 1 With right sides together, position 2-1/2-inch **BROWN** squares on 2 corners of the 6-1/2-inch **RED** square. Draw a diagonal line on the small squares; stitch on the lines, trim, and press. Repeat this process at the opposite corners of the **RED** square. <u>At this point the "apple" should measure 6-1/2-inches square.</u> Sew **BROWN** triangles to the left edge of the "apple" and to the top edge to make the base unit; press.

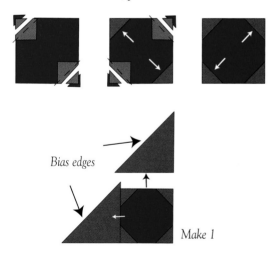

Bias edges

Make 1

Step 2 To prepare basket handle, fold 2 x 21-inch **RED** *bias* strip in half lengthwise, wrong sides together; press. To keep raw edges aligned, stitch a scant 1/4-inch from raw edges. Fold strip in half again so raw edges are hidden by first folded edge; press. At this point the handle should measure 1/2 x 21-inches.

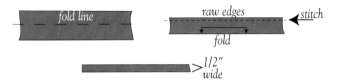

Step 3 Referring to diagram, pin handle on **BEIGE** triangle. Using matching thread, edge-stitch handle in place. Sew handle and base units together being careful not to stretch bias edges; press. At this point the basket block should measure 12-1/2-inches square.

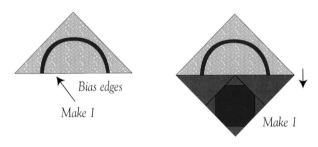

Bias edges

Make 1

Make 1

Step 4 Make a template using the leaf shape on page 31. Trace (2) leaves on the paper side of the fusible web leaving a small margin between each shape. Cut shapes apart.

Note: *Refer to **Paper-Backed Fusible Web Appliqué** on page 30 for complete instructions for appliquéing.*

Step 5 Place leaves on basket block; fuse in place and zigzag stitch using matching thread.

Make 1

Basket Block #3 Piecing

Note: *Refer to arrows on diagrams for pressing.*

Step 1 With right sides together, position 2-1/2-inch **BEIGE** squares on the corners of the 2-1/2 x 12-1/2-inch **GREEN #1** rectangle. Draw a diagonal line on the squares; stitch on the lines, trim, and press.

Make 1

Step 2 With right sides together, position a 2-1/2-inch **BEIGE** square on the top corner of a 2-1/2 x 4-1/2-inch **GREEN #1** rectangle. Draw a diagonal line on the square; stitch on the line, trim, and press. Make another unit reversing the direction of the stitching line. Sew the units together; press. Sew 4-1/2-inch **BEIGE** squares to both side edges of the unit; press. At this point the unit should measure 4-1/2 x 12-1/2-inches.

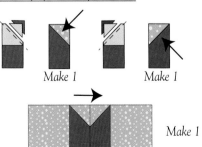

Make 1   Make 1

Make 1

Step 3 Sew the Step 1 unit to the bottom edge of the Step 2 unit; press. <u>At this point the unit should measure 6-1/2 x 12-1/2-inches.</u>

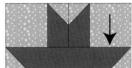

Step 2

Step 1

Make 1

Step 4 With right sides together, position a 4-1/2-inch **BLUE #1** square on the corner of a 6-1/2-inch **BEIGE** square. Draw a diagonal line on the small square; stitch on the line, trim, and press.

Make 2

Step 5 With right sides together, position a Step 4 pieced square on the corner of the 6-1/2 x 12-1/2-inch **BLUE #1** rectangle. Draw a diagonal line on the pieced square; stitch on the line, trim, and press. Repeat this process at the opposite corner of the rectangle. <u>At this point the basket base should measure 6-1/2 x 12-1/2-inches.</u>

Make 1

Step 6 Sew Step 3 unit and basket base together; press. <u>At this point the basket block should measure 12-1/2-inches square.</u>

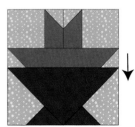

Make 1

Basket Block #4 Piecing

Note: *Refer to arrows on diagrams for pressing.*

Step 1 With right sides together, layer the 2-7/8-inch **GREEN #1** and **BEIGE** squares together. Press together, but do not sew. Cut the layered squares in half diagonally to make 2 sets of triangles. Stitch 1/4-inch from the diagonal edge of each pair of triangles; press. Sew the triangle-pieced squares together and sew a 2-1/2-inch **GREEN** square to the left edge; press. <u>At this point the unit should measure 2-1/2 x 6-1/2-inches.</u>

Make 2, 2-1/2-inch   *Make 1*
triangle-pieced squares

Step 2 With right sides together, position a 2-1/2-inch **BEIGE** square on the left corner of a 2-1/2 x 6-1/2-inch **GREEN #1** rectangle. Draw a diagonal line on the square; stitch on the line. Trim seam allowance to 1/4-inch; press. Repeat this process at the opposite corner of the rectangle. <u>At this point the unit should measure 2-1/2 x 6-1/2-inches.</u>

Make 1

Step 3 With right sides together, position a 2-1/2-inch **BEIGE** square on the left corner of a 2-1/2 x 4-1/2-inch **GREEN #1** rectangle. Draw a diagonal line on the square; stitch on the line, trim, and press. Repeat this process at the opposite corner of the rectangle. <u>At this point the unit should measure 2-1/2 x 4-1/2-inches.</u>

Make 1

Step 4 To make the trunk unit, position a 1-1/2-inch **BEIGE** square on the corner of a 2-1/2-inch **GREEN #1** square. Draw a diagonal line on the small square; stitch on the line, trim, and press. Repeat this process at the opposite corner of the large square. <u>At this point the trunk unit should measure 2-1/2-inches square.</u> Sew the Step 3 unit to the left edge of the trunk unit; press. <u>At this point the unit should measure 2-1/2 x 6-1/2-inches.</u>

Make 1

Step 5 Lay out the tree units, sew together; press. <u>At this point the tree block should measure 6-1/2-inches square.</u> Sew **RED** triangles to the left edge of tree block and to the top edge to make the base unit; press.

Step 1
Step 2
Step 4

Make 1

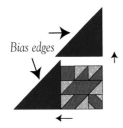

Bias edges

Step 6 To make the handle, sew 1-1/2 x 6-5/8-inch **RED** rectangles to the top/bottom edges of the 6-5/8-inch **BEIGE** square; press. Sew 1-1/2 x 8-5/8-inch **RED** rectangles to the side edges of the unit; press. Sew 2-5/8 x 8-5/8-inch **BEIGE** rectangles to the top/bottom edges of the

unit; press. Sew 2-5/8 x 12-7/8-inch **BEIGE** rectangles to the side edges of the unit; press. <u>At this point the square should measure 12-7/8-inches square.</u> Cut the square in half diagonally to make 2 triangles. One of the handle units will be used for basket block #7. Label the handle unit and set it aside.

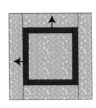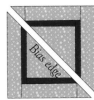

Set aside for Block #7 handle

Bias edge

Block #4 handle

Step 7 Sew handle and base units together being careful not to stretch the bias edges; press. <u>At this point the basket block should measure 12-1/2-inches square.</u>

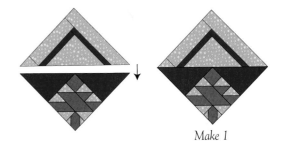

Make 1

25

Basket Block #5 Piecing

Note: *Refer to arrows on diagrams for pressing.*

Step 1 With right sides together, position a 2-1/2-inch **RED** square on the corner of the 2-1/2 x 4-1/2-inch **BEIGE** rectangle. Draw a diagonal line on the square; stitch on the line, trim, and press. Repeat this process at the opposite corner of the rectangle. Sew a 2-1/2-inch **BEIGE** square to the left edge of the unit; press. <u>At this point the unit should measure 2-1/2 x 6-1/2-inches.</u>

Make 1   *Make 1*

Step 2 With right sides together, position a 2-1/2-inch **BEIGE** square on the corner of the 2-1/2 x 6-1/2-inch **RED** rectangle. Draw a diagonal line on the square; stitch on the line, trim, and press. With right sides together, position a 2-1/2-inch **BEIGE** square on the corner of the 2-1/2 x 4-1/2-inch **RED** rectangle. Draw a diagonal line on the square; stitch on the line, trim, and press. Sew a 2-1/2-inch **GOLD** square to the bottom edge of the unit; press. <u>At this point each unit should measure 2-1/2 x 6-1/2-inches.</u>

Make 1   *Make 1*

Step 3 Sew together the Step 1 and 2 units; press. <u>At this point the block should measure 6-1/2-inches square.</u> Sew **GOLD** triangles to the left edge of the block and to the top edge to make the base unit; press.

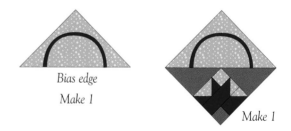

Make 1   Bias edges   *Make 1*

Step 4 To prepare basket handle, fold 2 x 21-inch **RED** *bias* strip in half lengthwise, wrong sides together; press. To keep raw edges aligned, stitch a scant 1/4-inch from raw edges. Fold strip in half again so raw edges are hidden by first folded edge; press. <u>At this point the handle should measure 1/2 x 21-inches.</u>

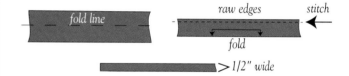

fold line   raw edges   stitch   fold   >1/2" wide

Step 5 Referring to diagram, pin handle on **BEIGE** triangle. Using matching thread, edge-stitch handle in place. Sew handle and base units together being careful not to stretch bias edges; press. <u>At this point the basket block should measure 12-1/2-inches square.</u>

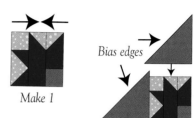

Bias edge
Make 1   *Make 1*

Block #6 Piecing

Note: Refer to arrows on diagrams for pressing.

Step 1   Sew together a 4-1/2-inch **GREEN #1** square, (2) 4-1/2-inch **BROWN** squares, and (3) **GREEN #1** triangles in horizontal rows; press. Sew rows together; press. Trim away excess fabric from **GREEN #1** triangles taking care to allow for a 1/4-inch seam allowance beyond the corners of the **BROWN** squares.

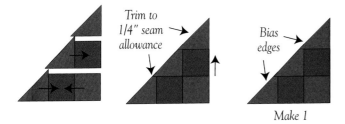

Trim to 1/4" seam allowance

Bias edges

Make 1

Step 2   To prepare basket handle, refer to **Basket Block #5** handle instructions (Step 4) using the 2 x 21-inch **GREEN #1** *bias* strip. <u>At this point the handle should measure 1/2 x 21-inches.</u>

fold line

raw edges   stitch

fold

1/2" wide

Step 3   Referring to diagram, pin handle on **BEIGE** triangle. Using matching thread, edge-stitch handle in place.

Make 1

Step 4   Make a template using the leaf shape on page 31. Trace (3) leaves on the paper side of the fusible web leaving a small margin between each shape. Cut shapes apart.

Note: *Refer to* **Paper-Backed Fusible Web Appliqué** *on page 30 for complete instructions for appliquéing.*

Step 5   Place leaves on handle unit; fuse in place and zigzag stitch using matching thread.

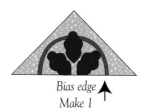

Bias edge
Make 1

Step 6   Sew handle and base units together being careful not to stretch bias edges; press. <u>At this point the block should measure 12-1/2-inches square.</u>

Make 1

Block #7 Piecing

Note: *Refer to arrows on diagrams for pressing.*

Step 1 Sew 2-5/8 x 4-5/8-inch **BLUE #3** rectangles to top/bottom edges of 4-5/8-inch **GOLD** square; press. Sew 2-5/8 x 8-3/4-inch **BLUE #3** rectangles to side edges; press. Sew 2-1/2 x 8-3/4-inch **RED** rectangles to top/bottom edges and sew 2-1/2 x 12-7/8-inch **RED** rectangles to side edges; press. <u>At this point the square should measure 12-7/8-inches square.</u> Cut the square in half diagonally to make 2 triangles. You will be using only 1 triangle for the base unit.

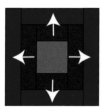

Make 1

Bias edge

Step 2 **Note:** *The handle unit was made with Block #4.* Sew handle and base units together being careful not to stretch bias edges; press. <u>At this point the block should measure 12-1/2-inches square.</u>

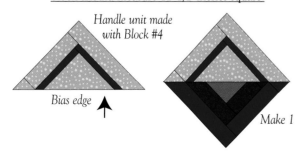

Handle unit made with Block #4

Bias edge

Make 1

Basket Block #8 Piecing

Note: *Refer to arrows on diagrams for pressing.*

Step 1 With right sides together, layer together 6-7/8-inch **RED** and **BEIGE** squares. Press together, but do not sew. Cut the layered square in half diagonally to make 2 sets of triangles. Stitch 1/4-inch from the diagonal edges of each pair of triangles; press. <u>At this point each triangle-pieced square should measure 6-1/2-inches square.</u>

Make 2, 6-1/2-inch triangle-pieced squares

Step 2 Position 5-1/2-inch **BEIGE** squares on the **RED** corner of the triangle-pieced squares. Draw a diagonal line on the **BEIGE** squares; stitch on the lines, trim, and press. Sew the units together to make the handle unit; press. <u>At this point the handle unit should measure 6-1/2 x 12-1/2-inches.</u>

Make 2   *Make 1*

Step 3 Position a 4-1/2-inch **RED** square on the corner of a 6-1/2-inch **BEIGE** square. Draw a diagonal line on the small square; stitch on the line, trim, and press.

Make 2

Step 4 Position a Step 3 unit on the corner of the 6-1/2 x 12-1/2-inch **BROWN** rectangle. Draw a diagonal line on the Step 3 unit; stitch on the line, trim, and press. Repeat this process at the opposite corner of the rectangle. <u>At this point the basket base should measure 6-1/2 x 12-1/2-inches.</u>

Make 1

Step 5 Sew together the handle and base units; press. <u>At this point the basket block should measure 12-1/2-inches square.</u>

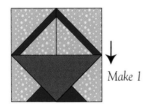

Make 1

Quilt Center

Cutting

From **GREEN PRINT #2**:
- Cut 2, 6-1/2 x 44-inch strips for spacers.
  From strips cut:
  5, 6-1/2 x 12-1/2-inch spacer rectangles

Quilt Center Assembly

Note: *Refer to arrows on diagrams for pressing.*

Step 1 Referring to the Quilt Center Assembly Diagram, lay out the blocks and spacer rectangles; sew them together in 3 vertical block rows and press. <u>At this point each block row should measure 12-1/2 x 42-1/2-inches.</u>

Step 2 Sew the block rows and the vertical lattice strips together; press. <u>At this point the quilt center should measure 48-1/2 x 42-1/2-inches.</u>

Step 3 Sew the top and bottom sections to the quilt center; press. <u>At this point the quilt center should measure 48-1/2 x 54-1/2-inches.</u>

Quilt Center Assembly Diagram

Paper-Backed Fusible Web Appliqué

Step 1 Make templates using the appliqué shapes. Trace the shapes on the paper side of the fusible web, leaving a small margin between each shape. Cut shapes apart.

Step 2 When you are fusing a large shape, fuse just the outer edges of the shape so that it will not look stiff when finished. To do this, draw a line about 3/8-inch inside the shape, and cut away the fusible web on this line.

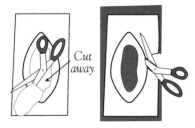

Cut away

Step 3 Following the manufacturer's instructions, fuse the shapes to the wrong side of the fabrics chosen for the appliqués. Let the fabric cool and cut along the traced line. Peel away the paper backing from the fusible web.

Note: *Use spray starch to make your appliqués more stable.*

Step 4 Place the shapes on the block; fuse in place. When machine appliquéing, we suggest pinning a square of tear-away stabilizer to the backside of the appliqué foundation triangle so it will lay flat when the appliqué is complete. We use extra-lightweight Easy Tear™ sheets as a stabilizer. Machine zigzag stitch around the shapes using matching thread. When the machine appliqué is complete, tear away the stabilizer. If you like, you could hand blanket stitch the shapes in place with pearl cotton.

Note: *To prevent the hand blanket stitches from "rolling off" the edges of the appliqué shapes, take an extra backstitch in the same place as you made the blanket stitch, going around the outer curves, corners, and points. For straight edges, taking a backstitch every inch is enough.*

Start   *Blanket Stitch*

Borders

Note: *Yardage given allows for border strips to be cut on the crosswise grain. Diagonally piece the strips as needed, referring to* **Diagonal Piecing** *instructions on page 140. Read through* **Border** *instructions on page 139 for general instructions on adding borders.*

Cutting

From **BLUE PRINT #3**:

• Cut 7, 6-1/2 x 44-inch outer border strips

• Cut 6, 2-1/2 x 44-inch inner border strips

From **RED PRINT**:

• Cut 7, 2-1/2 x 44-inch middle border strips

Attaching the Borders

Step 1 Attach the 2-1/2-inch wide **BLUE #3** inner border strips.

Step 2 Attach the 2-1/2-inch wide **RED** middle border strips.

Step 3 Attach the 6-1/2-inch wide **BLUE #3** outer border strips.

Putting It All Together

Cut the 4-1/8 yard length of backing fabric in half crosswise to make 2, 74-inch lengths. Refer to **Finishing the Quilt** on page 140 for complete instructions.

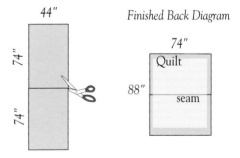

Finished Back Diagram

Quilting Suggestions:

- All **BEIGE**-small meander
- Blocks-in-the-ditch, echo, crosshatch, variety of Thimbleberries® stencils
- **GREEN #2** spacer rectangles-channel stitch
- **RED** spacer squares
  TB52—5-1/2" Oak Leaf
- **RED/BLUE** narrow borders (quilt as 1 border)
  TB 116—3-1/2" Leaf Wave
- **BLUE** outer border
  TB 111—5-1/2" Floral Vine

Binding

Cutting

From **RED DIAGONAL PRINT**:
- Cut 7, 2-3/4 x 44-inch strips

Sew binding to quilt using a 3/8-inch seam allowance. This measurement will produce a 1/2-inch wide finished double binding. Refer to **Binding and Diagonal Piecing** on page 140 for complete instructions.

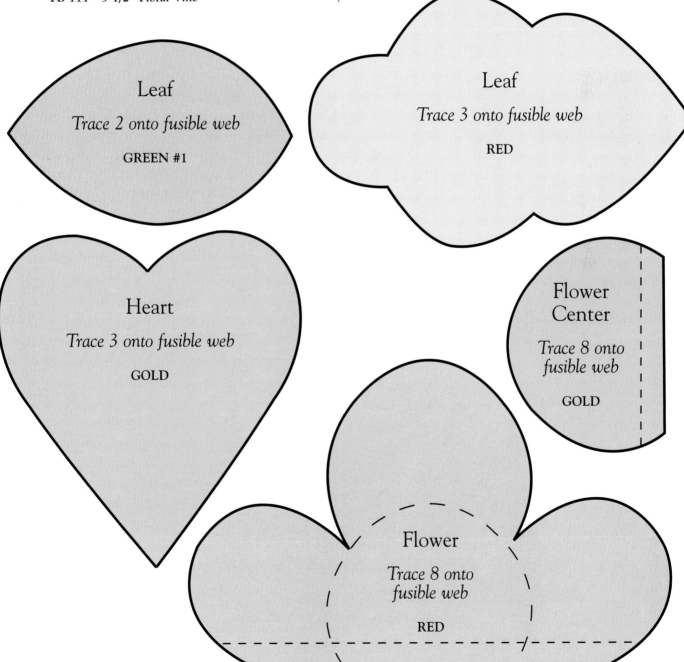

Leaf

Trace 2 onto fusible web

GREEN #1

Leaf

Trace 3 onto fusible web

RED

Heart

Trace 3 onto fusible web

GOLD

Flower Center

Trace 8 onto fusible web

GOLD

Flower

Trace 8 onto fusible web

RED

Basket Sampler Throw
68 x 74-inches

102 x 108-inches

To make a **Queen Size Basket Sampler**, follow the instructions beginning on page 17 to make the **Basket Sampler Throw** quilt top. After you have completed the top, follow the instructions below to piece and attach the flying geese and additional borders to make the **Queen** size quilt.

Fabrics & Supplies

To make the **Basket Sampler Queen Quilt**, purchase the additional border, binding, backing, and batting listed below. You _will not need_ the binding, backing, or batting listed for the **Throw Size** (68 x 74-inches) on page 17.

1-1/4 yards **BLUE PRINT #2** for flying geese border

2 yards **BEIGE PRINT** for background

2-3/4 yards **GREEN PRINT #2** for corner squares, outer border

3/4 yard **RED PRINT** for first middle border

7/8 yard **BLUE PRINT #3** for second middle border

1 yard **RED DIAGONAL PRINT** for binding

9 yards for 44-inch wide backing

OR

3-1/3 yards for 108-inch wide backing

quilt batting, at least 108 x 116-inches

Before beginning this project, read through **Getting Started** _on page 131._

Flying Geese Border

Cutting

From **BLUE PRINT #2**:
* Cut 16, 2-1/2 x 44-inch strips. From strips cut:
  142, 2-1/2 x 4-1/2-inch rectangles

From **BEIGE PRINT**:
* Cut 25, 2-1/2 x 44-inch strips. From strips cut:
  142, 2-1/2 x 4-1/2-inch rectangles
  142, 2-1/2-inch squares

From **GREEN PRINT #2**:
* Cut 1, 6-1/2 x 44-inch strip. From strip cut:
  4, 6-1/2-inch corner squares

Piecing

Note: _Refer to arrows on diagrams for pressing._

Step 1   With right sides together, position a 2-1/2 x 4-1/2-inch **BEIGE** rectangle on the left corner of a 2-1/2 x 4-1/2-inch **BLUE #2** rectangle. Draw a diagonal line on the **BEIGE** rectangle; stitch on the line. Trim seam allowance to 1/4-inch; press. Repeat this process at the right corner of the **BLUE #2** rectangle using a 2-1/2-inch **BEIGE** square. <u>At this point each flying geese unit should measure 2-1/2 x 6-1/2-inches.</u>

Make 72

Step 2   With right sides together, position a 2-1/2-inch **BEIGE** square on the left corner of a 2-1/2 x 4-1/2-inch **BLUE #2** rectangle. Draw a diagonal line on the square; stitch on the line. Trim seam allowance to 1/4-inch; press. Repeat this process at the right corner of the **BLUE #2** rectangle using a 2-1/2 x 4-1/2-inch **BEIGE** rectangle. <u>At this point each flying geese unit should measure 2-1/2 x 6-1/2-inches.</u>

Make 70

Step 3   For top/bottom borders, refer to Quilt Center Diagram for unit placement and sew together (17) Step 1 units and (17) Step 2 units; press. <u>At this point each flying geese border should measure 6-1/2 x 68-1/2-inches.</u> Sew flying geese borders to quilt center; press.

Step 4   For side borders, refer to Quilt Center Diagram for unit placement and sew together (19) Step 1 units and (18) Step 2 units; press. <u>At this point each flying geese border should measure 6-1/2 x 74-1/2-inches.</u> Sew 6-1/2-inch **GREEN #2** corner squares to the ends of both of the side flying geese borders; press. Sew flying geese borders to quilt center; press.

Quilt Center Diagram

Borders

Note: *Yardage given allows for border strips to be cut on the crosswise grain. Diagonally piece the strips as needed, referring to* **Diagonal Piecing** *instructions on page 140. Read through* **Border** *instructions on page 139 for general instructions on adding borders.*

Cutting

From **RED PRINT**:
- Cut 9, 2-1/2 x 44-inch first middle border strips

From **BLUE PRINT #3**:
- Cut 10, 2-1/2 x 44-inch second middle border strips

From **GREEN PRINT #2**:
- Cut 11, 7-1/2 x 44-inch outer border strips

Attaching the Borders

Note: *Refer to diagram on page 27 when adding borders.*

Step 1   Attach 2-1/2-inch wide **RED** first middle border strips.

Step 2   Attach 2-1/2-inch wide **BLUE #3** second middle border strips.

Step 3   Attach 7-1/2-inch wide **GREEN #2** outer border strips.

Putting It All Together

If you are using 108-inch wide backing fabric, trim the batting and backing so they are 6-inches larger than the quilt top. Refer to **Finishing the Quilt** on page 140 for complete instructions.

Note: *If you are using 44-inch wide backing fabric, cut the 9 yard length of backing fabric in thirds crosswise to make 3, 3 yard lengths. Refer to* **Finishing the Quilt** *on page 140 for complete instructions.*

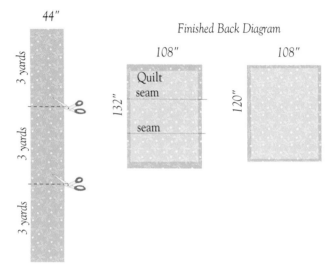

Quilting Suggestions:

- Refer to **Basket Sampler Throw** quilting suggestions on page 31.

- Flying geese border-small meander in **BEIGE**

- **GREEN** corner squares
  TB 52—5-1/2" Oak Leaf

- **RED/BLUE** narrow borders (quilt as 1 border)
  TB 116—3-1/2" Leaf Wave

- **GREEN** outer border
  TB 112—6-1/2" Floral Vine

Binding
Cutting

From **RED DIAGONAL PRINT**:
- Cut 11, 2-3/4 x 44-inch strips

Sew binding to quilt using a 3/8-inch seam allowance. This measurement will produce a 1/2-inch wide finished double binding. Refer to **Binding and Diagonal Piecing** on page 140 for complete instructions.

Apple Basket Wall Quilt

29-inches square

Fabrics & Supplies

3/8 yard **RED PRINT** for apple, handle, inner border

14-inch square **BEIGE PRINT** for background

1/3 yard **GREEN PRINT** for corner triangles, corner squares, leaf appliqués

7/8 yard **GOLD/CORAL FLORAL** for basket block, outer border

3/8 yard **GREEN PRINT** for binding

1 yard for backing

quilt batting, at least 35-inches square

paper-backed fusible web

tear-away fabric stabilizer (optional)

matching thread for appliqué

Before beginning this project, read through **Getting Started** *on page 131.*

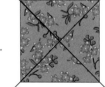

Basket Block

Cutting

From **RED PRINT**:
- Cut 1, 2 x 19-inch **bias** strip for basket handle
- Cut 1, 6-1/2-inch square

From **GOLD/CORAL FLORAL**:
- Cut 1, 9-3/4 x 44-inch strip. From strip cut: 1, 9-3/4-inch square. Cut the square diagonally into quarters to make 4 triangles. You will be using only 2 triangles.

9-3/4-inch square

- Cut 4, 2-1/2-inch squares

From **BEIGE PRINT**:
- Cut 1, 12-7/8-inch square. Cut the square in half diagonally to make 2 triangles. You will be using only 1 triangle.

12-7/8-inch square

Piecing

Note: Refer to arrows on diagrams for pressing.

Step 1   With right sides together, position 2-1/2-inch **GOLD/CORAL FLORAL** squares on 2 corners of the 6-1/2-inch **RED** square. Draw a diagonal line on the small squares; stitch on the lines. Trim seam allowances to 1/4-inch; press. Repeat this process at the opposite corners of the **RED** square. <u>At this point the "apple" should measure 6-1/2-inches square.</u>

Make 1

Step 2   Sew **GOLD/CORAL FLORAL** triangles to the left edge of the "apple" and to the top edge to make the base unit; press.

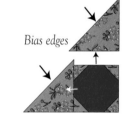

Bias edges

Step 3   To prepare the basket handle, fold the 2 x 19-inch **RED** *bias* strip in half lengthwise, wrong sides together; press. To keep raw edges aligned, stitch a scant 1/4-inch from the raw edges. Fold the strip in half again so raw edges are hidden by the first folded edge; press. <u>At this point the handle should measure 1/2 x 19-inches.</u>

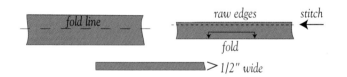

fold line   *raw edges*   *stitch*
fold
> 1/2" wide

Step 4   Referring to the diagram, pin the handle on the **BEIGE** triangle. Using matching thread, edge-stitch the handle in place.

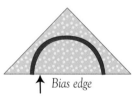

Bias edge

Step 5   Sew the handle and base units together being careful not to stretch the bias edges; press. <u>At this point the basket block should measure 12-1/2-inches square.</u>

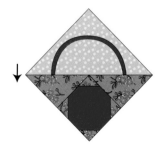

Paper-Backed Fusible Web Appliqué

Step 1 Make templates using the leaf shape on page 39. Trace (2) leaves on the paper side of the fusible web, leaving a small margin between each shape. Cut shapes apart.

Step 2 When you are fusing a large shape, like the leaf, fuse just the outer edges of the shape so that it will not look stiff when finished. To do this, draw a line about 3/8-inch inside the leaf, and cut away the fusible web on this line.

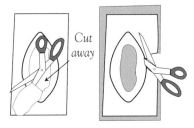

Step 3 Following the manufacturer's instructions, fuse the leaves to the wrong side of the fabric chosen for the appliqué. Let the fabric cool and cut along the traced line. Peel away the paper backing from the fusible web.

Note: Use spray starch to make your appliqués more stable.

Step 4 Place the leaves on the basket block; fuse in place. When machine appliquéing, pin a square of tear-away stabilizer to the backside of the block so it will lay flat when the appliqué is complete. We use extra-lightweight Easy Tear™ sheets as a stabilizer. Machine zigzag stitch around the shapes using matching thread. When the machine appliqué is complete, tear away the stabilizer. If you like, you could hand blanket stitch the shapes in place with pearl cotton.

Blanket Stitch
Start

Note: To prevent the hand blanket stitches from "rolling off" the edges of the appliqué shapes, take an extra backstitch in the same place as you made the blanket stitch, going around the outer curves, corners, and points. For straight edges, taking a backstitch every inch is enough.

Quilt Center and Borders

*Note: Yardage given allows for border strips to be cut on the crosswise grain. Diagonally piece strips as needed referring to **Diagonal Piecing** instructions on page 140. Read through **Border** instructions on page 139 for general instructions on adding borders.*

Cutting

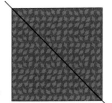

10-inch square corner triangles

From **GREEN PRINT**:
- Cut 1, 10 x 24-inch strip. From strip cut: 2, 10-inch squares. Cut the squares in half diagonally to make 4 corner triangles.
- Cut 4, 2-1/2-inch corner squares

From **RED PRINT**:
- Cut 2, 2-1/2 x 44-inch inner border strips

From **GOLD/CORAL FLORAL**:
- Cut 4, 4-1/2 x 44-inch outer border strips

Quilt Center Assembly and Attaching the Borders

Step 1 Sew 2 **GREEN** corner triangles to opposite edges of the basket block; press. Sew remaining corner triangles to the unit; press. Trim away excess fabric from the corner

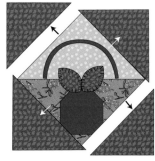

triangles leaving a 1/4-inch seam allowance beyond the block corners. Refer to **Trimming Side and Corner Triangles** for complete instructions.

Trimming Side and Corner Triangles

Begin at a corner by lining up your ruler 1/4-inch beyond the points of the block corners as shown. Cut along the edge of the ruler. Repeat this procedure on all four sides of the quilt top.

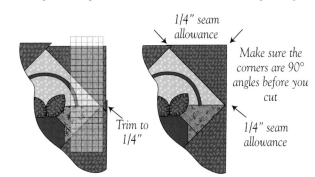

1/4" seam allowance

Make sure the corners are 90° angles before you cut

Trim to 1/4"

1/4" seam allowance

Step 2 Attach 2-1/2-inch wide **RED** top/bottom inner border strips. For side borders, measure quilt from top to bottom including seam allowances, but not the top/bottom borders just added. Cut the 2-1/2-inch wide **RED** side inner border strips to this length. Sew 2-1/2-inch **GREEN** corner squares to both ends of the side border strips; press. Attach the border strips to the quilt.

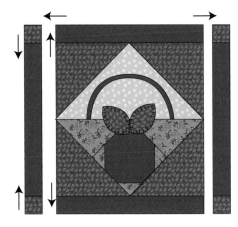

Step 3 Attach 4-1/2-inch wide **GOLD/CORAL FLORAL** outer border strips.

Putting It All Together

Trim the backing and batting so they are 6-inches larger than the quilt top. Refer to **Finishing the Quilt** on page 140 for complete instructions.

Leaf

Trace 2 onto fusible web

GREEN

Quilting Suggestions:

- "Apple"-TB23—5" Floral Burst

- Leaves-in-the-ditch & echo

- Basket-echo

- **BEIGE** background-stipple

- **GREEN** corner triangles-TB40—9" Corner Swirl

- Inner border/corner squares
  TB114—1-1/2" Leaf Wave

- Outer border-meander

Binding

Cutting

From **GREEN PRINT**:
- Cut 3, 2-3/4 x 44-inch strips

Sew binding to quilt using a 3/8-inch seam allowance. This measurement will produce a 1/2-inch wide finished double binding. Refer to **Binding and Diagonal Piecing** on page 140 for complete instructions.

Apple Basket
29-inches square

April Showers Table Runner

24 x 36-inches

Fabrics & Supplies

1/4 yard **DARK BLUE PRINT** for quilt center

1/4 yard **BEIGE PRINT** for quilt center

1/3 yard **PLUM PRINT**
for flower appliqués, inner border

1/4 yard **GREEN DOT** for flower center appliqués,
binding accent trim

1/2 yard **BLUE FLORAL** for outer border

3/8 yard **PLUM PRINT** for binding

3/4 yard for backing

quilt batting, at least 30 x 42-inches

paper-backed fusible web

tear-away fabric stabilizer (optional)

matching thread for appliqué

Before beginning this project, read through
Getting Started *on page 131.*

Flower Blocks

Makes 8 blocks

Cutting

From **DARK BLUE PRINT**:
- Cut 1, 6-7/8 x 44-inch strip.
  From strip cut:
  4, 6-7/8-inch squares.
  Cut the squares in half
  diagonally to make 8 triangles.

6-7/8-inch square

From **BEIGE PRINT**:
- Cut 1, 6-7/8 x 44-inch strip.
  From strip cut:
  4, 6-7/8-inch squares.
  Cut the squares in half
  diagonally to make 8 triangles.

6-7/8-inch square

Paper-Backed Fusible Web Appliqué

Step 1   Make templates using the flower shapes on page 43. Trace (8) flowers and flower centers on the paper side of the fusible web, leaving a small margin between each shape. Cut shapes apart.

Step 2   When you are fusing a large shape, like the flower, fuse just the outer edges of the shape so that it will not look stiff when finished. To do this, draw a line about 3/8-inch inside the flower, and cut away the fusible web on this line.

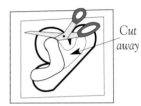

Cut away

Step 3   Following the manufacturer's instructions, fuse the flowers and flower centers to the wrong side of the fabrics chosen for the appliqués. Let the fabric cool and cut along the traced line. Peel away the paper backing from the fusible web.

Note: *Use spray starch to make your appliqués more stable.*

Step 4   Place the flowers and flower centers on the **BEIGE** triangles; fuse in place. When machine appliquéing, we suggest pinning a square of tear-away stabilizer to the backside of the appliqué foundation triangle so it will lay flat when the appliqué is complete. We use extra-lightweight Easy Tear™ sheets as a stabilizer. Machine zigzag stitch around the shapes using matching thread. When the machine appliqué is complete, tear away the stabilizer. If you like, you could hand blanket stitch the shapes in place with pearl cotton.

bias edge
Make 8

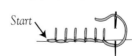

Blanket stitch

Start

Note: *To prevent the hand blanket stitches from "rolling off" the edges of the appliqué shapes, take an extra backstitch in the same place as you made the blanket stitch, going around the outer curves, corners, and points. For straight edges, taking a backstitch every inch is enough.*

Quilt Center Assembly

Note: Refer to arrows on diagrams for pressing.

Step 1   Sew together the appliquéd triangles and the **DARK BLUE** triangles in pairs; press.

*Make 8,
6-1/2-inch blocks*

Step 2   Sew together 4 of the blocks; press. Make 2 units. Sew the units together; press. <u>At this point the quilt center should measure 12-1/2 x 24-1/2-inches.</u>

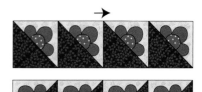

Make 1

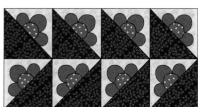

Make 1

Borders

*Note: Yardage given allows for border strips to be cut on the crosswise grain. Diagonally piece the strips as needed referring to **Diagonal Piecing** instructions on page 140. Read through **Border** instructions on page 139 for general instructions on adding borders.*

Cutting

From **PLUM PRINT**:
- Cut 3, 1-1/2 x 44-inch inner border strips

From **BLUE FLORAL**:
- Cut 3, 5-1/2 x 44-inch outer border strips

Attaching the Borders

Step 1   Attach 1-1/2-inch wide **PLUM** inner border strips.

Step 2   Attach 5-1/2-inch wide **BLUE FLORAL** outer border strips.

Putting It All Together

Trim backing and batting so they are 6-inches larger than the quilt top. Refer to **Finishing the Quilt** on page 140 for complete instructions.

Quilting Suggestions:

- Appliqué shapes-echo & in-the-ditch
- **BLUE** baskets-echo & in-the-ditch
- **BEIGE** background-stipple
- Inner border-in-the-ditch
- Outer border-meander

Accent Trim and Binding

Cutting

From **GREEN DOT**:
- Cut 4, 1 x 44-inch strips for accent trim

From **PLUM PRINT**:
- Cut 4, 2-3/4 x 44-inch binding strips

Attaching the Accent Trim

Step 1   With wrong sides together, fold the 1-inch wide **GREEN DOT** strips in half lengthwise; press. Aligning raw edges, machine baste an accent strip to 2 opposite side edges of the quilt with a 1/4-inch seam allowance. In the same manner, machine baste an accent strip to the remaining opposite side edges of the quilt. The ends of the accent strips will overlap at the corners; trim the ends.

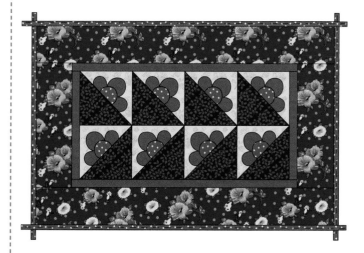

Step 2 Sew binding to the quilt using a 3/8-inch seam allowance. This measurement will produce a 1/2-inch wide finished double binding. Refer to **Binding and Diagonal Piecing** on page 140 for complete instructions. Approximately 1/4-inch of the **GREEN DOT** accent trim will be exposed once the binding is complete. You do not need to tack down the trim. The accent trim is narrow and it will lay flat, similar to a piping.

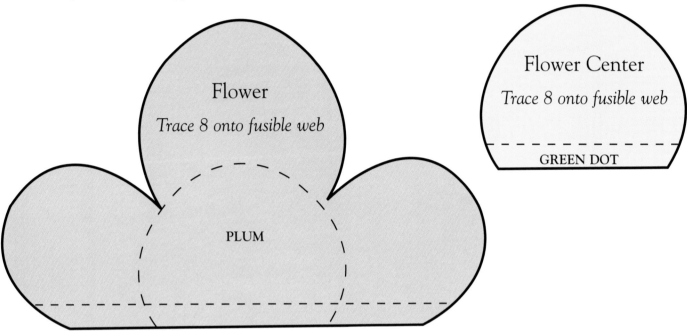

Flower

Trace 8 onto fusible web

PLUM

Flower Center

Trace 8 onto fusible web

GREEN DOT

April Showers
24 x 36-inches

Heart Basket Table Runner

20 x 30-inches

Heart Basket Table Runner

Fabrics & Supplies

1/4 yard **GREEN PRINT**
for basket handle, basket base

1/4 yard **BEIGE PRINT** for background

1/4 yard **ROSE PRINT** for basket, top band

8 x 16-inch rectangle **WINE PRINT**
for bottom band

6 x 44-inch rectangle **GOLD PRINT**
for heart appliqués, corner squares

1/3 yard **GREEN FLORAL** for outer border

1/3 yard **GREEN PRINT** for binding

3/4 yard for backing

quilt batting, at least 26 x 36-inches

paper-backed fusible web

tear-away fabric stabilizer (optional)

matching thread for appliqués

Before beginning this project, read through
Getting Started *on page 131.*

Basket Block

Cutting

From **GREEN PRINT**:
- Cut 1, 4-1/2 x 44-inch strip. From strip cut:
  2, 4-1/2-inch squares
  1, 2-7/8-inch square
  4, 2-1/2-inch squares

From **BEIGE PRINT**:
- Cut 1, 6-1/2 x 44-inch strip. From strip cut:
  2, 6-1/2-inch squares
  1, 4-1/2 x 6-1/2-inch rectangle
  1, 2-7/8-inch square
  4, 2-1/2 x 4-1/2-inch rectangles
  2, 2-1/2-inch squares

From **ROSE PRINT**:
- Cut 1, 6-1/2 x 12-1/2-inch rectangle

Piecing

Note: *Refer to arrows on diagrams for pressing.*

Step 1　With right sides together, position a 2-1/2-inch **GREEN** square on the upper left corner of a 4-1/2 x 6-1/2-inch **BEIGE** rectangle. Draw a diagonal line on the square; stitch on the line. Trim seam allowance to 1/4-inch; press. Repeat this process at the upper right corner of the rectangle.

Make 1

Step 2　With right sides together, position a 2-1/2-inch **GREEN** square on the corner of a 2-1/2 x 4-1/2-inch **BEIGE** rectangle. Draw a diagonal line on the square; stitch on the line, trim, and press. Repeat this process reversing the direction of the stitching line. Sew a 2-1/2-inch **BEIGE** square to the top edge of each of the units; press. Sew the units to both side edges of the Step 1 unit; press. At this point the unit should measure 6-1/2 x 8-1/2-inches.

   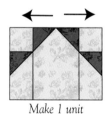

Make 1　　Make 1　　Make 1 unit

Step 3　With right sides together, layer the 2-7/8-inch **GREEN** and **BEIGE** squares. Press together, but do not sew. Cut the layered square in half diagonally to make 2 sets of triangles. Stitch 1/4-inch from the diagonal edge of each pair of triangles; press. Sew a 2-1/2 x 4-1/2-inch **BEIGE** rectangle to the top edge of each triangle-pieced square. At this point each unit should measure 2-1/2 x 6-1/2-inches.

Make 2,
2-1/2-inch
triangle-pieced squares　　Make 1　　Make 1

Step 4   Sew the Step 3 units to both side edges of the Step 2 unit; press. At this point the basket handle unit should measure 6-1/2 x 12-1/2-inches. Staystitch around the unit to secure the seams before adding the appliqué.

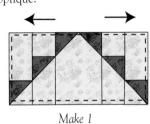

Make 1

Paper-Backed Fusible Web Appliqué

Step 1   Make template using the heart shape on page 47. Trace (3) hearts on the paper side of the fusible web, leaving a small margin between each shape. Cut shapes apart.

Step 2   When you are fusing a large shape, like the heart, fuse just the outer edges of the shape so that it will not look stiff when finished. To do this, draw a line about 3/8-inch inside the heart, and cut away the fusible web on this line.

Step 3   Following the manufacturer's instructions, fuse the hearts to the wrong side of the fabric chosen for the appliqué. Let the fabric cool and cut along the traced line. Peel away the paper backing from the fusible web.

Note: *Use spray starch to make your appliqués more stable.*

Step 4   Place the hearts on the handle unit; fuse in place. When machine appliquéing, pin a square of tear-away stabilizer to the backside of the block so it will lay flat when the appliqué is complete. We use extra-lightweight Easy Tear™ sheets as a stabilizer. Machine zigzag stitch around the shapes using matching thread. When the machine appliqué is complete, tear away the stabilizer. If you like, you could hand blanket stitch the shapes in place with pearl cotton.

 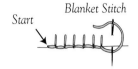

Start   *Blanket Stitch*

Note: *To prevent the hand blanket stitches from "rolling off" the edges of the appliqué shapes, take an extra backstitch in the same place as you made the blanket stitch, going around the outer curves, corners, and points. For straight edges, taking a backstitch every inch is enough.*

Step 5   With right sides together, position a 4-1/2-inch **GREEN** square on the corner of a 6-1/2-inch **BEIGE** square. Draw a diagonal line on the small square; stitch on the line, trim, and press.

Make 2

Step 6   With right sides together, position a Step 5 unit on the corner of the 6-1/2 x 12-1/2-inch **RED** rectangle. Draw a diagonal line on the pieced unit; stitch on the line, trim, and press. Repeat this process at the opposite corner of the rectangle. At this point the basket base should measure 6-1/2 x 12-1/2-inches.

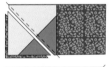 

Make 1

Step 7   Sew together the basket handle and basket base units; press. At this point the basket block should measure 12-1/2-inches square.

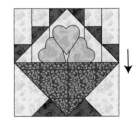

Borders

Note: *Yardage given allows for border strips to be cut on the crosswise grain. Diagonally piece the strips as needed referring to the **Diagonal Piecing** instructions on page 140. Read through **Border** instructions on page 139 for general instructions on adding borders.*

Cutting

From **ROSE PRINT**:
- Cut 1, 4-1/2 x 12-1/2-inch top band

From **WINE PRINT**:
- Cut 1, 6-1/2 x 12-1/2-inch bottom band

From **GREEN FLORAL**:
- Cut 2, 4-1/2 x 44-inch outer border strips

From **GOLD PRINT**:
- Cut 4, 4-1/2-inch corner squares

Attaching the Borders

Step 1   Attach 4-1/2 x 12-1/2-inch **ROSE** top band; press. Attach 6-1/2 x 12-1/2-inch wide **WINE** bottom band; press.

Step 2   Attach 4-1/2-inch wide **GREEN FLORAL** top/bottom borders. For side borders, measure quilt from top to bottom including seam allowances, but not the top/bottom borders just added. Cut the 4-1/2-inch wide **GREEN FLORAL**  side border strips to this length. Sew 4-1/2-inch **GOLD** corner squares to both ends of the side border strips; press. Attach the border strips to the quilt.

Putting It All Together

Trim the backing and batting so they are 6-inches larger than the quilt top. Refer to ***Finishing the Quilt*** on page 140 for complete instructions.

Quilting Suggestions:

- Heart appliqués-in-the-ditch & echo
- Basket-1/2 of **TB85**—7-1/2" Heart Swirl
- Basket base-echo
- **BEIGE** background-stipple
- **ROSE** top band-**TB79**—3-1/2" Mirrored Spring
- **WINE** bottom band-**TB42**—8" x 6" Mirrored Spring
- Border/corner squares-**TB107**—3-1/2" Ivy Vine

Binding

Cutting

From **GREEN PRINT**:
- Cut 3, 2-3/4 x 44-inch strips

Sew binding to quilt using a 3/8-inch seam allowance. This measurement will produce a 1/2-inch wide finished double binding. Refer to ***Binding and Diagonal Piecing*** on page 140 for complete instructions.

Heart

Trace 3 onto fusible web

GOLD

Heart Basket
20 x 30-inches

Pine Tree Basket Wall Quilt

43-inches square

Fabrics & Supplies

1/2 yard **RED PRINT** for basket block, inner border, berry appliqués

3/4 yard **CREAM FLORAL** for basket block, wide middle border

3/8 yard **GREEN PRINT** for basket block, narrow middle border, leaf/vine appliqués

1/3 yard **BEIGE PRINT** for corner triangles

1 yard **GREEN/RED FLORAL** for outer border

1/2 yard **RED PRINT** for binding

2-3/4 yards for backing

quilt batting, at least 49-inches square

paper-backed fusible web

tear-away fabric stabilizer (optional)

matching thread for appliqué

Before beginning this project, read through **Getting Started** *on page 131.*

Basket Block
Cutting

From **RED PRINT**:
- Cut 1, 9-3/4 x 44-inch strip. From strip cut: 1, 9-3/4-inch square. Cut the square diagonally into quarters to make 4 triangles. You will be using only 2 triangles.

9-3/4-inches square

- Cut 1, 1-1/2 x 8-5/8-inch rectangle
- Cut 1, 1-1/2 x 6-5/8-inch rectangle

From **CREAM FLORAL**:
- Cut 1, 6-5/8 x 44-inch strip. From strip cut:
  1, 6-5/8-inch square
  1, 2-7/8-inch square
  1, 2-5/8 x 8-5/8-inch rectangle
  1, 2-5/8 x 12-7/8-inch rectangle
  4, 2-1/2-inch squares
  2, 1-1/2-inch squares

From **GREEN PRINT**:
- Cut 1, 2-7/8 x 44-inch strip. From strip cut:
  1, 2-7/8-inch square
  1, 2-1/2 x 6-1/2-inch rectangle
  1, 2-1/2 x 4-1/2-inch rectangle
  2, 2-1/2-inch squares

Piecing

Note: *Refer to arrows on diagrams for pressing.*

Step 1 With right sides together, layer the 2-7/8-inch **GREEN** and **CREAM FLORAL** squares together. Press together, but do not sew. Cut the layered squares in half diagonally to make 2 sets of triangles. Stitch 1/4-inch from the diagonal edge of each pair of triangles; press. Sew the triangle-pieced squares together and sew a 2-1/2-inch **GREEN** square to the left edge; press. <u>At this point the unit should measure 2-1/2 x 6-1/2-inches.</u>

 Make 1

Make 2, 2-1/2-inch triangle-pieced squares

Step 2 With right sides together, position a 2-1/2-inch **CREAM FLORAL** square on the left corner of a 2-1/2 x 6-1/2-inch **GREEN** rectangle. Draw a diagonal line on the square; stitch on the line. Trim seam allowance to 1/4-inch; press. Repeat this process at the opposite corner of the rectangle. <u>At this point the unit should measure 2-1/2 x 6-1/2-inches.</u>

Make 1

Step 3   With right sides together, position a 2-1/2-inch **CREAM FLORAL** square on the left corner of a 2-1/2 x 4-1/2-inch **GREEN** rectangle. Draw a diagonal line on the square; stitch on the line, trim, and press.

Make 1

Step 4   To make the trunk unit, position a 1-1/2-inch **CREAM FLORAL** square on the corner of a 2-1/2-inch **GREEN** square. Draw a diagonal line on the small square; stitch on the line, trim, and press. Repeat this process at the opposite corner of the large square. <u>At this point the trunk unit should measure 2-1/2-inches square.</u> Sew the Step 3 unit to the left edge of the trunk unit; press. <u>At this point the unit should measure 2-1/2 x 6-1/2-inches.</u>

Make 1   Make 1
trunk unit

Step 5   Lay out the leaf units, sew together; press. <u>At this point the leaf block should measure 6-1/2-inches square.</u>

Step 6   Sew a **RED** triangle to the left edge of leaf block and sew a **RED** triangle to the top edge to make the base unit; press.

Step 7   To make the handle, sew the 1-1/2 x 6-5/8-inch **RED** rectangles to the top/bottom edges of the 6-5/8-inch **CREAM FLORAL** square; press. Sew the 1-1/2 x 8-5/8-inch **RED** rectangles to the side edges of the unit; press. Sew the 2-5/8 x 8-5/8-inch **CREAM FLORAL** rectangles to the top/bottom edges of the unit; press. Sew the 2-5/8 x 12-7/8-inch **CREAM FLORAL** rectangles to the side edges of the unit; press. <u>At this point the square should measure 12-7/8-inches square.</u> Cut the square in half diagonally to make 2 triangles. You will be using only 1 triangle for the basket handle.

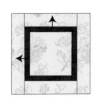

Make 1

Step 8   Sew the handle and base units together being careful not to stretch the bias edges; press. <u>At this point the basket block should measure 12-1/2-inches square.</u>

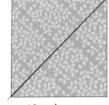

Make 1

Quilt Center and Borders

Note: The corner triangles are larger than necessary and will be trimmed before the borders are attached. Yardage given allows for border strips to be cut on the crosswise grain. Diagonally piece strips as needed referring to **Diagonal Piecing** *instructions on page 140. Read through* **Border** *instructions on page 139 for general instructions on adding borders.*

Cutting

From **BEIGE PRINT**:
• Cut 1, 10 x 44-inch strip.
  From strip cut: 2, 10-inch squares.
  Cut the squares in half diagonally
  to make 4 corner triangles.

10-inch square corner triangles

From **RED PRINT**:
• Cut 2, 2-1/2 x 44-inch inner border strips

From **CREAM FLORAL**:
• Cut 4, 4-1/2 x 44-inch wide middle border strips

From **GREEN PRINT**:
• Cut 4, 1-1/2 x 44-inch narrow middle border strips

From **GREEN/RED FLORAL**:
• Cut 5, 6-1/2 x 44-inch outer border strips

Assembling and Attaching the Borders

Step 1 Sew 2 of the **BEIGE** corner triangles to opposite edges of the basket block; press. Sew the remaining corner triangles to the unit; press. Trim away the excess fabric from the corner triangles, leaving a 1/4-inch seam allowance beyond the block corners. Refer to *Trimming Side and Corner Triangles* instructions on page 136.

Step 2 Attach 2-1/2-inch wide **RED** inner border strips.

Step 3 Attach 4-1/2-inch wide **CREAM FLORAL** wide middle border strips.

Step 4 Attach 1-1/2-inch wide **GREEN PRINT** narrow middle border strips.

Step 5 Attach 6-1/2-inch wide **GREEN/RED FLORAL** outer border strips.

Vine Appliqué

Cutting

From **GREEN PRINT**:
- Cut enough 1-3/8-inch wide *bias* strips to make (4) 27-inch long strips. Diagonally piece the strips together as needed.

Appliqué the Vines

Step 1 Fold each 1-3/8-inch wide **GREEN** *bias* strip in half lengthwise, wrong sides together; press. To keep raw edges aligned, stitch a scant 1/4-inch away from the raw edges. Fold each strip in half again so raw edges are hidden by the first folded edge; press. At this point each vine should measure 3/8 x 27-inches.

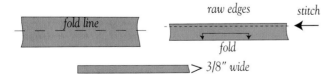

Step 2 Using the vine placement curve on page 52, position the prepared vines on the **BEIGE** middle border; pin in place. We suggest hand basting the

vines in a zigzag fashion which makes appliquéing so much easier. Using matching thread, edge-stitch the vines in place.

Basting Diagram

Paper-Backed Fusible Web Appliqué

Step 1 Make templates using the leaf and berry shapes on page 53. Trace (24) leaves and (24) berries on the paper side of the fusible web, leaving a small margin between each shape. Cut shapes apart.

Step 2 When you are fusing a large shape, like the leaf, fuse just the outer edges of the shape so that it will not look stiff when finished. To do this, draw a line about 3/8-inch inside the leaf, and cut away the fusible web on this line.

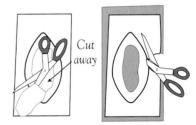

Cut away

Step 3 Following the manufacturer's instructions, fuse the leaves and berries to the wrong side of the fabrics chosen for the appliqués. Let the fabric cool and cut along the traced line. Peel away the paper backing from the fusible web.

Note: Use spray starch to make your appliqués more stable.

Step 4 Place the leaves and berries on the border; fuse in place. When machine appliquéing, we suggest pinning a square of tear-away stabilizer to the backside of the block so it will lay flat when the appliqué is complete. Machine zigzag stitch around the shapes using matching thread. When the machine appliqué is complete, tear away the stabilizer. If you like, you could hand blanket stitch the shapes in place with pearl cotton.

Blanket Stitch

Start

Note: *To prevent the hand blanket stitches from "rolling off" the edges of the appliqué shapes, take an extra backstitch in the same place as you made the blanket stitch, going around the outer curves, corners, and points. For straight edges, taking a backstitch every inch is enough.*

Putting It All Together

Cut the 2-3/4 yard length of backing fabric in half crosswise to make 2, 1-3/8 yard lengths. Refer to **Finishing the Quilt** on page 140 for complete instructions.

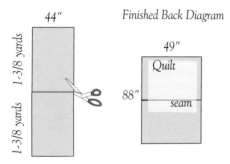

Finished Back Diagram

Quilting Suggestions:

- Tree-in-the-ditch & echo

- Tree background-stipple

- **RED** basket base-1" crosshatching

- Handle unit:
  RED-in-the-ditch and through the middle
  CREAM triangle-**TB 49—7" Corner Heart**
  CREAM background-stipple

- **BEIGE** corner triangles-**TB 39—9" Triangle Trail**

- **RED** border-**TB 64—1-1/2" Nordic Scroll**

- **GREEN** leaves-in-the-ditch

- **CREAM** border-stipple

- **GREEN** and **GREEN/RED FLORAL** borders-meander as 1 border

Binding

Cutting

From **RED PRINT**:
- Cut 5, 2-3/4 x 44-inch strips

Sew binding to quilt using a 3/8-inch seam allowance. This measurement will produce a 1/2-inch wide finished double binding. Refer to **Binding and Diagonal Piecing** on page 140 for complete instructions.

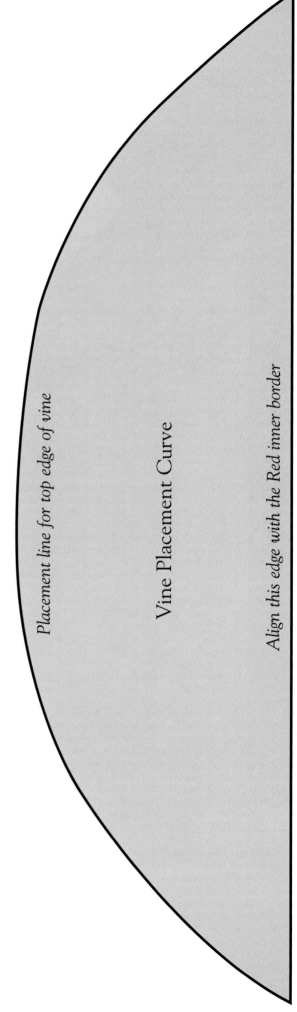

Placement line for top edge of vine

Vine Placement Curve

Align this edge with the Red inner border

Berry

*Trace 24
onto fusible web*

RED

Leaf

Trace 24 onto fusible web

GREEN

Pine Tree Basket

43-inches square

Winter Spruce Quilt

74 x 85-inches

Fabrics & Supplies

1/3 yard *each* of 6 GREEN PRINTS
for pine tree blocks

5/8 yard GOLD PRINT for double hourglass blocks

4-1/2 yards BEIGE PRINT for background,
side/corner triangles, border

1-1/2 yards RED PRINT for lattice segments

1/2 yard BLACK PRINT for lattice post squares

3/4 yard RED PRINT for binding

5 yards for backing

quilt batting, at least 80 x 90-inches

Before beginning this project, read through
Getting Started *on page 131.*

Pine Tree Blocks

*Makes a total of 30 blocks -
5 from each GREEN PRINT*

Cutting

From *each* of the 6 GREEN PRINTS:

• Cut 1, 2-7/8 x 44-inch strip

• Cut 2, 2-1/2 x 44-inch strips. From strips cut:
5, 2-1/2 x 6-1/2-inch rectangles
5, 2-1/2 x 4-1/2-inch rectangles
10, 2-1/2-inch squares

From BEIGE PRINT:

• Cut 3, 2-7/8 x 44-inch strips

• Cut 8, 2-1/2 x 44-inch strips. From strips cut:
120, 2-1/2-inch squares

• Cut 3, 1-1/2 x 44-inch strips. From strips cut:
60, 1-1/2-inch squares

Piecing

Note: *Refer to arrows on diagrams for pressing.*

Note: *The following instructions are for **one** of the GREEN PRINTS. When you have* <u>five blocks</u> *made using this GREEN PRINT, repeat the instructions for the remaining GREEN PRINTS.*

Step 1 With right sides together, layer the 2-7/8 x 44-inch GREEN and BEIGE strips together. Press together, but do not sew. Cut the layered strip into squares. Cut the layered squares in half diagonally to make 10 sets of triangles. Stitch 1/4-inch from the diagonal edge of each pair of triangles; press. Sew the triangle-pieced squares together and sew a 2-1/2-inch GREEN square to the left edge; press. <u>At this point each unit should measure 2-1/2 x 6-1/2-inches.</u>

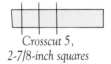

Crosscut 5,
2-7/8-inch squares   Make 10,
2-1/2-inch
triangle-pieced squares   Make 5

Step 2 With right sides together, position a 2-1/2-inch BEIGE square on the left corner of a 2-1/2 x 6-1/2-inch GREEN rectangle. Draw a diagonal line on the square; stitch on the line. Trim seam allowance to 1/4-inch; press. Repeat this process at the opposite corner of the rectangle. <u>At this point each unit should measure 2-1/2 x 6-1/2-inches.</u>

Make 5

Step 3 With right sides together, position a 2-1/2-inch BEIGE square on the left corner of a 2-1/2 x 4-1/2-inch GREEN rectangle. Draw a diagonal line on the square; stitch on the line, trim, and press. Repeat this process at the opposite corner of the rectangle.

Make 5

Step 4 To make the trunk unit, position a 1-1/2-inch BEIGE square on the corner of a 2-1/2-inch GREEN square. Draw a diagonal line on the small square; stitch on the line, trim, and press. Repeat this process at the opposite corner of the large square. <u>At this point the trunk unit</u>

should measure 2-1/2-inches square. Sew the Step 3 unit to the left edge of the trunk unit; press. <u>At this point each unit should measure 2-1/2 x 6-1/2-inches.</u>

Make 5
trunk units

Make 5

Step 5 Lay out the tree units, sew together; press. <u>At this point each pine tree block should measure 6-1/2-inches square.</u>

Step 1
Step 2
Step 4

Make 5 blocks from
each GREEN PRINT

Step 6 Using the remaining **GREEN PRINTS**, repeat Steps 1 through 5 to make a total of 30 pine tree blocks.

Double Hourglass Blocks

Makes 20 blocks

Cutting

From **GOLD PRINT**:

- Cut 3, 2-7/8 x 44-inch strips

- Cut 3, 2-1/2 x 44-inch strips. From strips cut: 40, 2-1/2-inch squares

From **BEIGE PRINT**:

- Cut 3, 2-7/8 x 44-inch strips

- Cut 4, 2-1/2 x 44-inch strips. From strips cut: 60, 2-1/2-inch squares

Piecing

Note: *Refer to arrows on diagrams for pressing.*

Step 1 With right sides together, layer the 2-7/8 x 44-inch **GOLD** and **BEIGE** strips together in pairs. Press together, but do not sew. Cut the layered strips into squares. Cut the layered squares in half diagonally to make 80 sets of triangles. Stitch 1/4-inch from the diagonal edge of each pair of triangles; press.

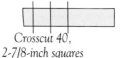

Crosscut 40,
2-7/8-inch squares

Make 80,
2-1/2-inch
triangle-pieced squares

Step 2 Referring to block diagram for placement, sew together the triangle-pieced squares, and the 2-1/2-inch **GOLD** and **BEIGE** squares in rows; press. Sew the rows together; press. <u>At this point each double hourglass block should measure 6-1/2-inches square.</u>

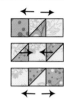

Make 20 blocks

Quilt Center and Border

Note: *The side/corner triangles are larger than necessary and will be trimmed before the border is attached. Yardage given allows for lattice/border strips to be cut on the crosswise grain. Diagonally piece strips as needed referring to* **Diagonal Piecing** *instructions on page 140. Read through* **Border** *instructions on page 139 for general instructions on adding borders.*

Cutting

From **RED PRINT**:

- Cut 20, 2-1/2 x 44-inch strips. From strips cut: 120, 2-1/2 x 6-1/2-inch lattice segments

From **BLACK PRINT**:

- Cut 5, 2-1/2 x 44-inch strips. From strips cut: 71, 2-1/2-inch lattice post squares

From **BEIGE PRINT**:

- Cut 9, 7-1/2 x 44-inch border strips

- Cut 2, 14 x 44-inch strips. From strips cut: 5, 14-inch squares. Cut the squares diagonally into quarters to make 20 triangles. You will be using only 18 for side triangles.

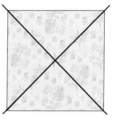

14-inch square
side triangles

- Cut 1, 10 x 44-inch strip. From strip cut: 2, 10-inch squares. Cut the squares in half diagonally to make 4 corner triangles.

10-inch square
corner triangles

Quilt Center Assembly

Note: *Press seam allowances toward lattice segments and side/corner triangles.*

Step 1   Refer to Quilt Center Assembly Diagram for placement. Sew together 2-1/2 x 6-1/2-inch **RED** lattice segments and pieced blocks as shown to make the block rows; press.

Step 2   Sew together 2-1/2-inch **BLACK** lattice post squares and 2-1/2 x 6-1/2-inch **RED** lattice segments to make the lattice strips; press.

Step 3   Sew the lattice strips and block rows together; press.

Important Note: Pay attention to row #6. *Sew together 9 pieced blocks and 10 lattice segments; press. Sew together 10 **BLACK** lattice post squares and 9 **RED** lattice segments; press. Sew this lattice strip to the <u>bottom edge</u> of the block row; press. Sew a side triangle to the <u>right edge</u> of the block row; press. Sew together 11 **BLACK** lattice post squares and 10 **RED** lattice segments; press. Sew this lattice strip to the <u>top edge</u> of the block row; press.*

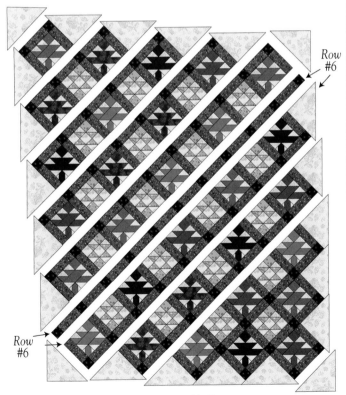

Quilt Center Assembly Diagram

Row #6 (labeled near top right of diagram)

Row #6 (labeled near bottom left of diagram)

Step 4   Sew remaining side triangles to the ends of the block rows/lattice strips; press.

Step 5   Pin rows together at block intersections; sew rows together and press.

Step 6   Sew corner triangles to quilt center; press.

Step 7   Trim away excess fabric from side and corner triangles taking care to allow a 1/4-inch seam allowance beyond the corners of each lattice post square. Refer to *Trimming Side and Corner Triangles* for complete instructions.

Trimming Side and Corner Triangles

Begin at a corner by lining up your ruler 1/4-inch beyond the points of the lattice post corners as shown. Cut along the edge of the ruler. Repeat this procedure on all four sides of the quilt top.

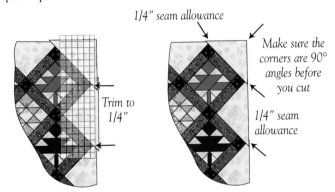

1/4" seam allowance

Trim to 1/4"

Make sure the corners are 90° angles before you cut

1/4" seam allowance

Step 8   Attach 7-1/2-inch wide **BEIGE** border strips.

Putting It All Together

Cut the 5 yard length of backing fabric in half crosswise to make 2, 2-1/2 yard lengths. Refer to **Finishing the Quilt** on page 140 for complete instructions.

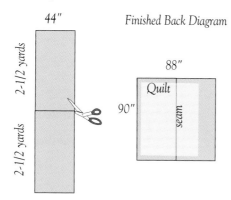

Finished Back Diagram

Quilting Suggestions:

- Tree blocks-in-the-ditch
- **GOLD** blocks-TB 17—5" Lady Slipper
- Lattice strips-in-the-ditch

- Side triangles-TB 49—9" Corner Hearts
- Corner triangles-TB 49—7" Corner Hearts
- Outer border-TB 44—5-1/2" Star Vine Border
- Meander behind stencil on side/corner triangles/border

Binding
Cutting

From **RED PRINT**:
- Cut 8, 2-3/4 x 44-inch strips

Sew binding to quilt using a 3/8-inch seam allowance. This measurement will produce a 1/2-inch wide finished double binding. Refer to **Binding and Diagonal Piecing** on page 140 for complete instructions.

Winter Spruce
74 x 85-inches

Sunrise

Lynette invites you to see how color
choices change the look of quilt creations.

From a summery Sunrise Quilt to a bed-sized
Wedding Quilt and floral Spring Fling Throw,
Lynette shows you how the fabrics you choose
for the same block take you through seasons and
celebrations—always with confidence when
blending Thimbleberries® colorways.

Sunrise Throw

62 x 76-inches

Fabrics & Supplies for the Blocks

Block 1

1/8 yard **MEDIUM GREEN PRINT**

1/8 yard **DARK GREEN PRINT**

3 x 44-inch piece **BEIGE PRINT**

1/8 yard **LIGHT ROSE PRINT**

5 x 44-inch piece **DARK ROSE PRINT**

Block 2

6 x 12-inch piece **MEDIUM BLUE PRINT**

6 x 18-inch piece **ROSE PRINT**

1/8 yard **DARK BLUE PRINT**

1/8 yard **BEIGE PRINT**

Block 3

8-inch square **GREEN/YELLOW FLORAL**

8 x 20-inch piece **ROSE PRINT**

5 x 20-inch piece **BEIGE PRINT**

5 x 20-inch piece **GREEN PRINT**

5-inch square **GOLD PRINT**

Block 4

4 x 22-inch piece **GREEN PRINT**

7 x 42-inch piece **GOLD PRINT**

4 x 20-inch piece **PURPLE FLORAL**

4 x 44-inch piece **BEIGE PRINT**

6-inch square **PURPLE FLORAL**

Block 5

6 x 18-inch piece **GREEN PRINT**

4 x 21-inch piece **MEDIUM BLUE PRINT**

4 x 42-inch piece **DARK BLUE PRINT**

4 x 20-inch piece **GOLD PRINT**

4 x 42-inch piece **BEIGE PRINT**

Block 6

5 x 10-inch piece **MEDIUM PLUM PRINT**

5 x 10-inch piece **GOLD FLORAL**

1/8 yard **DARK PLUM PRINT**

1/8 yard **BEIGE PRINT**

5 x 16-inch piece **GREEN PRINT**

Fabrics & Supplies for Finishing the Quilt

1-1/2 yards **BEIGE FLORAL**
for hourglass blocks, inner/middle borders

2/3 yard **GOLD PRINT #1**
for hourglass blocks, pieced lattice

1/4 yard **DARK BLUE PRINT** for hourglass blocks

1-1/2 yards **LARGE GREEN FLORAL** for outer border

5/8 yard **GREEN PRINT** for pieced lattice/border

1/3 yard **ROSE PRINT** for pieced border

1/3 yard **GOLD PRINT #2** for pieced border

5/8 yard **GREEN PRINT** for binding

4 yards for backing

quilt batting, at least 68 x 82-inches

Before beginning this project, read through
Getting Started *on page 131.*

Sunrise Block 1

Cutting

From **MEDIUM GREEN PRINT**:
- Cut 1, 2-1/2 x 44-inch strip.
  From strip cut:
  4, 2-1/2 x 5-1/2-inch rectangles

From **DARK GREEN PRINT**:
- Cut 1, 2-1/2 x 44-inch strip. From strip cut:
  4, 2-1/2-inch squares
  8, 1-1/2-inch squares

From **BEIGE PRINT**:
- Cut 1, 1-1/2 x 44-inch strip. From strip cut:
  24, 1-1/2-inch squares

From **LIGHT ROSE PRINT**:
- Cut 1, 2-1/2-inch square

- Cut 1, 1-1/2 x 28-inch strip. From strip cut:
  16, 1-1/2-inch squares

From **DARK ROSE PRINT**:
- Cut 1, 2-1/2 x 44-inch strip. From strip cut:
  8, 2-1/2 x 3-1/2-inch rectangles

- Cut 1, 1-1/2 x 44-inch strip. From strip cut:
  20, 1-1/2-inch squares

Piecing

Note: *Refer to arrows on diagrams for pressing.*

Step 1　Referring to the diagram, sew together the 1-1/2-inch **DARK ROSE** and **LIGHT ROSE** squares to make a nine-patch unit. <u>At this point each nine-patch unit should measure 3-1/2-inches square.</u>

Make 8　
Make 4　

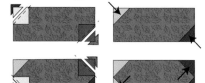

Make 4 nine-patch units

Step 2　With right sides together, position a 1-1/2-inch **BEIGE** square on the upper left corner of a 2-1/2 x 5-1/2-inch **MEDIUM GREEN** rectangle. Draw a diagonal line on the square; stitch on the line. Trim seam allowance to 1/4-inch; press. Position a 1-1/2-inch **DARK GREEN** square on the lower right corner of the rectangle. Draw a diagonal line on the square; stitch on the line, trim, and press. Referring to the diagram, repeat this process at the opposite corners of the rectangle.

Make 4

Step 3　With right sides together, position 1-1/2-inch **BEIGE** squares on the upper corners of a 2-1/2 x 3-1/2-inch **DARK ROSE** rectangle. Draw a diagonal line on the squares; stitch on the lines, trim, and press. Make 8 sub-units. Sew a sub-unit to the left edge of a Step 1 nine-patch unit; press. Make 4 units. Sew a sub-unit to the right edge of a 2-1/2-inch **DARK GREEN** square; press. Make 4 units. Sew the units together in pairs; press. <u>At this point each heart unit should measure 5-1/2-inches square.</u>

  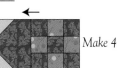

Make 8 sub-units　*Make 4*

Make 4　　*Make 4 heart units*

Step 4 Sew Step 3 heart units to both side edges of a Step 2 unit; press.

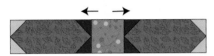

Make 2

Step 5 Sew Step 2 units to both side edges of a 2-1/2-inch **LIGHT ROSE** square; press.

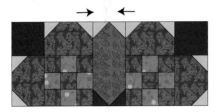

Make 1

Step 6 Sew Step 4 units to the top/bottom edges of the Step 5 unit; press. At this point the block should measure 12-1/2-inches square.

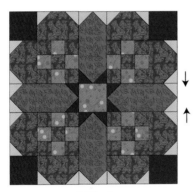

Make 1

Sunrise Block 2

Cutting

From **MEDIUM BLUE PRINT**:
- Cut 2, 4-7/8-inch squares

From **ROSE PRINT**:
- Cut 2, 4-7/8-inch squares

- Cut 2, 2-7/8-inch squares

From **DARK BLUE PRINT**:
- Cut 8, 2-7/8-inch squares

From **BEIGE PRINT**:
- Cut 6, 2-7/8-inch squares

- Cut 4, 2-1/2-inch squares

Piecing

Note: *Refer to arrows on diagrams for pressing.*

Step 1 With right sides together, layer (6) 2-7/8-inch **DARK BLUE** and **BEIGE** squares together in pairs. Press together, but do not sew. Cut the layered squares diagonally in half to make 12 sets of triangles. Stitch 1/4-inch from the diagonal edge of each pair of triangles; press.

   Make 12, 2-1/2-inch triangle-pieced squares

Step 2 With right sides together, layer (2) 2-7/8-inch **DARK BLUE** and **ROSE** squares together in pairs. Press together, but do not sew. Cut the layered

65

squares diagonally in half to make 4 sets of triangles. Stitch 1/4-inch from the diagonal edge of each pair of triangles; press.

Make 4, 2-1/2-inch triangle-pieced squares

Step 3 With right sides together, layer the 4-7/8-inch **MEDIUM BLUE** and **ROSE** squares together in pairs. Press together, but do not sew. Cut the layered squares diagonally in half to make 4 sets of triangles. Stitch 1/4-inch from the diagonal edge of each pair of triangles; press.

Make 4, 4-1/2-inch triangle-pieced squares

Step 4 Sew a Step 1 triangle-pieced square to the right edge of a Step 2 triangle-pieced square; press. Make 4 units. Sew the units to the bottom edge of the Step 3 triangle-pieced squares; press. <u>At this point each unit should measure 4-1/2 x 6-1/2-inches.</u>

Make 4   *Make 4*

Step 5 Sew together the remaining Step 1 triangle-pieced squares in pairs; press. Sew 2-1/2-inch **BEIGE** squares to the end of each unit; press. Make 4 units. Sew the units to the right edge of the Step 4 units; press. <u>At this point each unit should measure 6-1/2-inches square.</u>

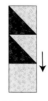 

Make 4   *Make 4*

Step 6 Referring to the block diagram, sew together the Step 5 units in pairs; press. Sew the pairs together; press. <u>At this point the block should measure 12-1/2-inches square.</u>

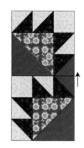 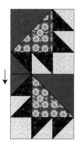 

Make 1

Sunrise Block 3

Cutting

From **GREEN/ FLORAL**:
- Cut 1, 6-7/8-inch square

From **ROSE PRINT**:
- Cut 1, 6-7/8-inch square
- Cut 3, 3-7/8-inch squares

From **BEIGE PRINT**:
- Cut 3, 3-7/8-inch squares
- Cut 2, 3-1/2-inch squares

From **GREEN PRINT**:
- Cut 2, 3-1/2 x 9-1/2-inch rectangles

From **GOLD PRINT**:
- Cut 1, 3-1/2-inch square

Piecing

Note: *Refer to arrows on diagrams for pressing.*

Step 1   With right sides together, layer the 6-7/8-inch **GREEN/YELLOW FLORAL** and **ROSE** squares together. Press together, but do not sew. Cut the layered square in half diagonally to make 2 sets of triangles. You will be using only 1 set of triangles. Stitch 1/4-inch from the diagonal edge of 1 pair of triangles; press.

Make 1, 6-1/2-inch triangle-pieced square

Step 2   With right sides together, layer the 3-7/8-inch **BEIGE** and **ROSE** squares together in pairs. Press together, but do not sew. Cut the layered squares in half diagonally to make 6 sets of triangles. You will be using only 5 sets of triangles. Stitch 1/4-inch from the diagonal edge of each pair of triangles; press.

Make 5, 3-1/2-inch triangle-pieced squares

Step 3   Sew (2) Step 2 triangle-pieced squares together; press. Sew the unit to the top edge of the Step 1 triangle-pieced square; press. Sew (3) Step 2 triangle-pieced squares together; press. Sew the unit to the left edge of the Step 1 unit; press. At this point the unit should measure 9-1/2-inches square.

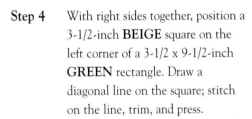

Make 1

Step 4   With right sides together, position a 3-1/2-inch **BEIGE** square on the left corner of a 3-1/2 x 9-1/2-inch **GREEN** rectangle. Draw a diagonal line on the square; stitch on the line, trim, and press.

Make 1

Step 5   With right sides together, position a 3-1/2-inch **BEIGE** square on the right corner of a 3-1/2 x 9-1/2-inch **GREEN** rectangle. Draw a diagonal line on the square; stitch on the line, trim, and press. Sew the 3-1/2-inch **GOLD** square to the left edge of the unit; press. At this point the unit should measure 3-1/2 x 12-1/2-inches.

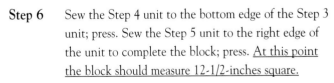

Make 1

Step 6   Sew the Step 4 unit to the bottom edge of the Step 3 unit; press. Sew the Step 5 unit to the right edge of the unit to complete the block; press. At this point the block should measure 12-1/2-inches square.

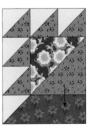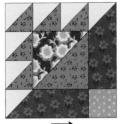

Make 1

Sunrise Block 4

Cutting

From **GREEN PRINT**:
- Cut 8, 2-1/2-inch squares

From **GOLD PRINT**:
- Cut 6, 2-7/8-inch squares

- Cut 1, 2-1/2 x 44-inch strip. From strip cut:
  4, 2-1/2 x 4-1/2-inch rectangles
  8, 2-1/2-inch squares

From **PURPLE FLORAL**:
- Cut 6, 2-7/8-inch squares

From **BEIGE PRINT**:
- Cut 1, 2-1/2 x 44-inch strip. From strip cut:
  4, 2-1/2 x 4-1/2-inch rectangles
  4, 2-1/2-inch squares

From **PURPLE PRINT**:
- Cut 1, 4-1/2-inch square

Piecing

Note: *Refer to arrows on diagrams for pressing.*

Step 1 With right sides together, position a 2-1/2-inch **GREEN** square on the corner of a 2-1/2 x 4-1/2-inch **GOLD** rectangle. Draw a diagonal line on the square; stitch on the line, trim, and press. Repeat this process at the opposite corner of the rectangle.

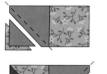

Make 4

Step 2 With right sides together, position a 2-1/2-inch **GOLD** square on the corner of a 2-1/2 x 4-1/2-inch **BEIGE** rectangle. Draw a diagonal line on the square; stitch on the line, trim, and press. Repeat this process at the opposite corner of the rectangle.

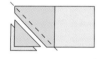

Make 4

Step 3 Sew the Step 1 and Step 2 units together in pairs; press. <u>At this point each unit should measure 4-1/2-inches square.</u>

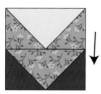

Make 4

Step 4 With right sides together, layer the 2-7/8-inch **PURPLE FLORAL** and **GOLD** squares together in pairs. Press together, but do not sew. Cut the layered squares in half diagonally to make 12 sets of triangles. Stitch 1/4-inch from the diagonal edge of each pair of triangles; press.

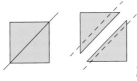

Make 12, 2-1/2-inch triangle-pieced squares

Step 5 Referring to the diagram, sew together (3) triangle-pieced squares and a 2-1/2-inch **BEIGE** square; press. <u>At this point each unit should measure 4-1/2-inches square.</u>

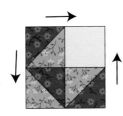

Make 4

Step 6 Sew the Step 3 units to the top/bottom edges of the 4-1/2-inch **PURPLE PRINT** square; press. Sew the Step 5 units to both side edges of the remaining Step 3 units; press. Sew the units to the side edges of the square unit; press. <u>At this point the block should measure 12-1/2-inches square.</u>

 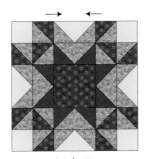

Make 1

Sunrise Block 5

Cutting

From **GREEN PRINT**:

• Cut 1, 4-1/2-inch square

• Cut 4, 2-1/2-inch squares

From **MEDIUM BLUE PRINT**:

• Cut 8, 2-1/2-inch squares

From **DARK BLUE PRINT**:

• Cut 1, 2-1/2 x 44-inch strip. From strip cut: 16, 2-1/2-inch squares

From **GOLD PRINT**:

• Cut 4, 2-1/2 x 4-1/2-inch rectangles

From **BEIGE PRINT**:

• Cut 1, 2-1/2 x 44-inch strip. From strip cut: 4, 2-1/2 x 4-1/2-inch rectangles 8, 2-1/2-inch squares

Piecing

Note: *Refer to arrows on diagrams for pressing.*

Step 1 With right sides together, position 2-1/2-inch **MEDIUM BLUE** squares on opposite corners of the 4-1/2-inch **GREEN** square. Draw diagonal lines on the small squares; stitch on the lines, trim, and press. Repeat this process at the opposite corners of the large square.

Make 1

Step 2 With right sides together, position a 2-1/2-inch **DARK BLUE** square on the corner of a 2-1/2 x 4-1/2-inch **GOLD** rectangle. Draw a diagonal line on the square; stitch on the line, trim, and press. Repeat this process at the opposite corner of the rectangle.

    Make 4

Step 3 With right sides together, position a 2-1/2-inch **DARK BLUE** square on the corner of a 2-1/2 x 4-1/2-inch **BEIGE** rectangle. Draw a diagonal line on the square; stitch on the line, trim, and press. Repeat this process at the opposite corner of the rectangle.

    Make 4

Step 4 Sew the Step 2 and Step 3 units together in pairs; press seams open. At this point each pair should measure 4-1/2-inches square.

 Make 4

Step 5 Referring to the diagram, sew together (2) 2-1/2-inch **BEIGE** squares, (1) 2-1/2-inch **MEDIUM BLUE** square, and (1) 2-1/2-inch **GREEN** square; press. At this point each unit should measure 4-1/2-inches square.

 *Make 4*

Step 6 Sew Step 4 units to the top/bottom edges of the Step 1 unit; press. Sew Step 5 units to both side edges of the remaining Step 4 units; press. Sew the units to the side edges of the Step 1 unit; press. At this point the block should measure 12-1/2-inches square.

 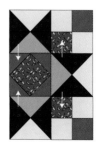 

Make 1

Sunrise Block 6

Cutting

From **MEDIUM PLUM PRINT**:
- Cut 2, 3-7/8-inch squares

From **GOLD FLORAL**:
- Cut 2, 3-7/8-inch squares

From **DARK PLUM PRINT**:
- Cut 1, 2 x 44-inch strip. From strip cut: 16, 2-inch squares

From **BEIGE PRINT**:
- Cut 1, 3-1/2 x 44-inch strip. From strip cut: 16, 2 x 3-1/2-inch rectangles

From **GREEN PRINT**:
- Cut 4, 3-1/2-inch squares

Piecing

Note: *Refer to arrows on diagrams for pressing.*

Step 1 With right sides together, layer (2) 3-7/8-inch **MEDIUM PLUM** and **GOLD FLORAL** squares together in pairs. Press together, but do not sew. Cut the layered squares in half diagonally to make 4 sets of triangles. Stitch 1/4-inch from the diagonal edge of each pair of triangles; press.

Make 4, 3-1/2-inch triangle-pieced squares

Step 2 Sew the triangle-pieced squares together in pairs; press. Sew the pairs together; press. <u>At this point the pinwheel unit should measure 6-1/2-inches square.</u>

Make 2

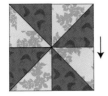

Make 1

Step 3 With right sides together, position a 2-inch **DARK PLUM** square on the corner of a 2 x 3-1/2-inch **BEIGE** rectangle. Draw a diagonal line on the square; stitch on the line, trim, and press. Make 16 units. Sew units together to make (4) 4-piece units; press. <u>At this point each 4-piece unit should measure 3-1/2 x 6-1/2-inches.</u>

Make 16   *Make 4 units*

Step 4 Sew 4-piece units to the top/bottom edges of the pinwheel unit; press. Sew 3-1/2-inch **GREEN** squares to both ends of the remaining Step 3 units; press. Sew the units to the side edges of the pinwheel unit; press. <u>At this point the block should measure 12-1/2-inches square.</u>

Make 1

Quilt Center

Note: *Yardage given allows for border strips to be cut on crosswise grain. Diagonally piece strips as needed referring to* **Diagonal Piecing** *on page 140. Read through* **Border** *instructions on page 139 for general instructions on adding borders.*

Cutting

From **BEIGE FLORAL**:
- Cut 2, 7-1/4 x 44-inch strips. From strips cut: 6, 7-1/4-inch squares
- Cut 5, 2-1/2 x 44-inch inner border strips

From **GOLD PRINT #1**:
- Cut 2, 7-1/4 x 44-inch strips. From strips cut: 8, 7-1/4-inch squares
- Cut 1, 4-1/2 x 44-inch strip. From strip cut: 4, 4-1/2 x 6-1/2-inch rectangles

From **DARK BLUE PRINT**:
- Cut 1, 7-1/4 x 44-inch strip. From strip cut: 2, 7-1/4-inch squares

From **GREEN PRINT**:
- Cut 4, 4-1/2 x 44-inch strips. From strips cut: 22, 4-1/2 x 6-1/2-inch rectangles

From **ROSE PRINT**:
- Cut 2, 4-1/2 x 44-inch strips. From strips cut: 8, 4-1/2 x 6-1/2-inch rectangles

From **GOLD PRINT #2**:
- Cut 2, 4-1/2 x 44-inch strips. From strips cut: 8, 4-1/2 x 6-1/2-inch rectangles

Quilt Center Assembly

Step 1 To make the **BEIGE/GOLD #1** hourglass blocks, with right sides together, layer (6) 7-1/4-inch **BEIGE** and **GOLD #1** squares in pairs. Press together, but do not sew. Cut the layered squares diagonally into quarters to make 24 sets of triangles. Stitch along the same bias edge of each pair of triangles being careful not to stretch the triangles; press. Sew the triangle units together in pairs to make the hourglass blocks; press. <u>At this point each hourglass block should measure 6-1/2-inches square.</u>

Bias edges

Make 24 triangle units   *Make 12 hourglass blocks*

71

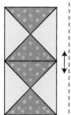

Step 2   Sew (6) Step 1 hourglass blocks together in pairs to make 3 vertical lattice strips; press. Referring to the quilt diagram on page 61 for block placement, sew the pieced blocks to both side edges of the vertical lattice strips; press. <u>At this point each block row should measure 12-1/2 x 30-1/2-inches.</u>

Make 3 vertical lattice strips

Step 3   Sew together (3) 4-1/2 x 6-1/2-inch **GREEN** rectangles and (2) 4-1/2 x 6-1/2-inch **GOLD #1** rectangles; press. Make 2 lattice strips. <u>At this point each lattice strip should measure 4-1/2 x 30-1/2-inches.</u>

Make 2 lattice strips

Step 4   Referring to the quilt diagram on page 73, sew together the 3 block rows and the 2 lattice strips to make the quilt center; press. <u>At this point the quilt center should measure 30-1/2 x 44-1/2-inches.</u>

Step 5   Attach 2-1/2-inch wide **BEIGE FLORAL** inner border strips.

Step 6   For the top/bottom pieced borders, sew together (3) **BEIGE/GOLD #1** hourglass blocks and (4) 4-1/2 x 6-1/2-inch **GREEN** rectangles; press. Make 2 pieced border strips. <u>At this point each pieced border should measure 6-1/2 x 34-1/2-inches.</u> Sew pieced border strips to top/bottom edges of quilt center; press.

Step 7   To make the **DARK BLUE/GOLD #1** hourglass blocks, with right sides together, layer (2) 7-1/4-inch **DARK BLUE** and **GOLD #1** squares in pairs. Press together, but do not sew. Cut the layered squares diagonally into quarters to make 8 sets of triangles. Stitch along the same bias edge of each pair of triangles; press. Sew the triangle units together in pairs to make the hourglass blocks; press. <u>At this point each hourglass block should measure 6-1/2-inches square.</u>

Bias edges

Make 8 triangle units

Make 4 hourglass blocks

Step 8   For the side pieced borders, sew together (4) each of the 4-1/2 x 6-1/2-inch **GREEN, ROSE,** and **GOLD #2** rectangles; press. Make 2 pieced border strips. Sew **DARK BLUE/GOLD #1** hourglass blocks to both ends of the pieced borders; press. <u>At this point each pieced border should measure 6-1/2 x 60-1/2-inches.</u> Sew the pieced border strips to the side edges of the quilt center; press.

Middle/Outer Borders

*Note: Yardage given allows for border strips to be cut on crosswise grain. Diagonally piece strips as needed referring to **Diagonal Piecing** on page 140. Read through **Border** instructions on page 139 for general instructions on adding borders.*

Cutting

From **BEIGE FLORAL**:
- Cut 7, 2-1/2 x 44-inch middle border strips

From **LARGE GREEN FLORAL**:
- Cut 7, 6-1/2 x 44-inch outer border strips

Attaching the Borders

Step 1   Attach 2-1/2-inch wide **BEIGE FLORAL** middle border strips.

Step 2   Attach 6-1/2-inch wide **LARGE GREEN FLORAL** outer border strips.

Putting It All Together

Cut the 4 yard length of backing fabric in half crosswise to make 2, 2 yard lengths. Refer to **Finishing the Quilt** on page 140 for complete instructions.

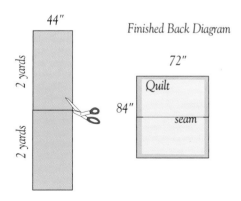

Finished Back Diagram

Quilting Suggestions:

- Pieced blocks-
  TB2—11" **Loop-d-Loop**
  TB18—11" **Lady Slipper**
  TB8—11" **Leaf Quartet**
  TB87—11-1/2" **Heart Swirl**
  TB14—11" **Bur Oak**
  TB10—11" **Radish Top**

- Vertical lattice-**TB111**—5-1/2" **Floral Vine**

- Horizontal lattice-channel stitch

- Pieced border-**TB44**—5-1/2" **Star Vine Border**

- **BEIGE** narrow borders-**TB64**—1-1/2" **Nordic Scroll**

- Outer border-**TB111**—5-1/2" **Floral Vine**

Binding
Cutting

From **GREEN PRINT**:
- Cut 7, 2-3/4 x 44-inch strips

Sew binding to quilt using a 3/8-inch seam allowance. This measurement will produce a 1/2-inch wide finished double binding. Refer to ***Binding and Diagonal Piecing*** on page 140 for complete instructions.

Sunrise Throw
62 x 76-inches

Wedding Quilt

91 x 108-inches

Fabrics & Supplies

2-1/2 yards **PLUM PRINT**
for pieced blocks, inner border

2/3 yard **BEIGE/PLUM PRINT**
for pieced blocks

1 yard **GREEN PRINT** for pieced blocks

3/4 yard **RUST PRINT** for pieced blocks

2-1/4 yards **BEIGE PRINT**
for pieced blocks, alternate blocks

1-1/2 yards **LIGHT GOLD PRINT**
for side/corner triangles

2-3/4 yards **PLUM/GOLD FLORAL**
for outer border

1 yard **RUST PRINT** for binding

8-5/8 yards of 44-inch wide backing

OR

3-1/4 yards of 108-inch wide backing

quilt batting, at least 97 x 114-inches

Before beginning this project, read through
Getting Started *on page 131.*

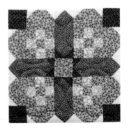

Blocks

Makes 20 blocks

Cutting

From **PLUM PRINT**:
- Cut 2, 2-1/2 x 44-inch strips.
  From strips cut:
  20, 2-1/2-inch squares

- Cut 14 more 2-1/2 x 44-inch strips. From strips cut:
  160, 2-1/2 x 3-1/2-inch rectangles

- Cut 15, 1-1/2 x 44-inch strips

From **BEIGE/PLUM PRINT**:
- Cut 12, 1-1/2 x 44-inch strips

From **GREEN PRINT**:
- Cut 12, 2-1/2 x 44-inch strips. From strips cut:
  80, 2-1/2 x 5-1/2-inch rectangles

From **RUST PRINT**:
- Cut 5, 2-1/2 x 44-inch strips. From strips cut:
  80, 2-1/2-inch squares

- Cut 6, 1-1/2 x 44-inch strips. From strips cut:
  160, 1-1/2-inch squares

From **BEIGE PRINT**:
- Cut 18, 1-1/2 x 44-inch strips. From strips cut:
  480, 1-1/2-inch squares

Piecing

Note: *Refer to arrows on diagrams for pressing.*

Step 1   Aligning long edges, sew
1-1/2 x 44-inch **PLUM** strips
to both side edges of a
1-1/2 x 44-inch **BEIGE/PLUM**
PRINT strip. Make 6 strip sets.

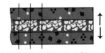

*Crosscut 160, 1-1/2-inch
wide segments*

Press referring to **Hints and Helps for Pressing Strip
Sets.** Cut strip sets into segments.

Hints and Helps for Pressing Strip Sets

When sewing strips of fabric together for strip
sets, it is important to press the seam allowances
nice and flat, usually to the dark fabric. Be
careful not to stretch as you press, causing a
"rainbow effect." This will affect the accuracy

*Avoid this
"rainbow effect"*

and shape of the pieces cut from the strip set. Press on the wrong side
first with the strips perpendicular to the ironing board. Flip the piece
over and press on the right side to prevent little pleats from forming
at the seams. Laying the strip set lengthwise on the ironing board
seems to encourage the rainbow effect.

Step 2 Aligning long edges, sew 1-1/2 x 44-inch **BEIGE/PLUM PRINT** strips to both side edges of a 1-1/2 x 44-inch **PLUM** strip. Make 3 strip sets; press. Cut strip sets into segments.

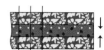

Crosscut 80, 1-1/2-inch wide segments

Step 3 Sew Step 1 segments to both side edges of the Step 2 segments to make nine-patch units; press. At this point each nine-patch unit should measure 3-1/2-inches square.

Make 80

Step 4 With right sides together, position a 1-1/2-inch **BEIGE** square on the upper left corner of a 2-1/2 x 5-1/2-inch **GREEN** rectangle. Draw a diagonal line on the square; stitch on the line. Trim seam allowance to 1/4-inch; press. Position a 1-1/2-inch **RUST** square on the lower right corner of the rectangle. Draw a diagonal line on the square; stitch on the line, trim, and press. Referring to the diagram, repeat this process at the opposite corners of the rectangle.

Make 80

Step 5 With right sides together, position 1-1/2-inch **BEIGE** squares on the upper corners of a 2-1/2 x 3-1/2-inch **PLUM** rectangle. Draw a diagonal line on the squares; stitch on the lines, trim, and press. Make 160 sub-units. Sew a sub-unit to the left edge of a Step 3 nine-patch unit; press. Make 80 units. Sew a sub-unit to the right edge of a 2-1/2-inch **RUST** square; press. Make 80 units. Sew the units together to make heart units; press. At this point each heart unit should measure 5-1/2-inches square.

Make 160 sub-units

Make 80 *Make 80*

Make 80 heart units

Step 6 Sew Step 5 heart units to both side edges of the Step 4 units; press. At this point each unit should measure 5-1/2 x 12-1/2-inches.

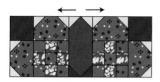

Make 40

Step 7 Sew Step 4 units to both side edges of the 2-1/2-inch **PLUM** squares; press. At this point each unit should measure 2-1/2 x 12-1/2-inches.

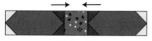

Make 20

Step 8 Sew the Step 6 units to the top/bottom edges of the Step 7 units; press. At this point each block should measure 12-1/2-inches square.

Step 6

Step 7

Step 6

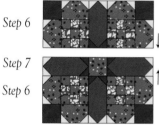

Make 20 blocks

Quilt Center

Note: Side and corner triangles are larger than necessary and will be trimmed before borders are added.

Cutting

From **BEIGE PRINT**:
- Cut 4, 12-1/2 x 44-inch strips. From strips cut: 12, 12-1/2-inch alternate block squares

From **LIGHT GOLD PRINT**:
- Cut 2, 19 x 44-inch strips. From strips cut: 4, 19-inch squares. Cut the squares diagonally into quarters for a total of 16 triangles. You will be using only 14 for side triangles.

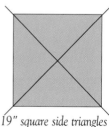

19" square side triangles

- Cut 1, 11 x 44-inch strip. From strip cut: 2, 11-inch squares. Cut the squares in half diagonally to make 4 corner triangles.

11" square corner triangles

Quilt Center Assembly

Step 1   Referring to Quilt Center Assembly Diagram for block placement, sew the pieced blocks, alternate blocks, and side/corner triangles together in 8 diagonal rows. Press seam allowances toward side triangles and alternate blocks so the seams will fit snugly together with less bulk.

Step 2   Pin the rows together at the block intersections; sew the rows together and press.

Step 3   Sew remaining corner triangles to quilt center; press.

Step 4   Trim away excess fabric from side and corner triangles taking care to allow a 1/4-inch seam allowance beyond the corners of each block. Refer to *Trimming Side and Corner Triangles* for complete instructions.

Quilt Center Assembly Diagram

Trimming Side and Corner Triangles

Begin at a corner by lining up your ruler 1/4-inch beyond the points of the block corners as shown. Cut along the edge of the ruler. Repeat this procedure on all four sides of the quilt top.

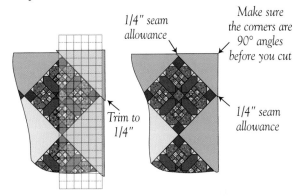

1/4" seam allowance

Make sure the corners are 90° angles before you cut

Trim to 1/4"

1/4" seam allowance

Borders

Note: *Yardage given allows for border strips to be cut on the crosswise grain. Diagonally piece strips as needed, referring to* **Diagonal Piecing** *instructions on page 140. Read through* **Border** *instructions on page 139 for general instructions on adding borders.*

Cutting

From **PLUM PRINT**:
- Cut 9, 2-1/2 x 44-inch inner border strips

From **PLUM/GOLD FLORAL**:
- Cut 10, 9-1/2 x 44-inch outer border strips

Attaching the Borders

Step 1   Attach 2-1/2-inch wide **PLUM** inner border strips.

Step 2   Attach 9-1/2-inch wide **PLUM/GOLD FLORAL** outer border strips.

Putting It All Together

If you are using 108-inch wide backing fabric, trim the batting and backing so they are 6-inches larger than the quilt top. Refer to **Finishing the Quilt** on page 140 for complete instructions.

Note: *If you are using 44-inch wide backing fabric, cut the 8-5/8 yard length of backing fabric in thirds crosswise to make 3, 2-7/8 yard lengths. Refer to* **Finishing the Quilt** *on page 140 for complete instructions.*

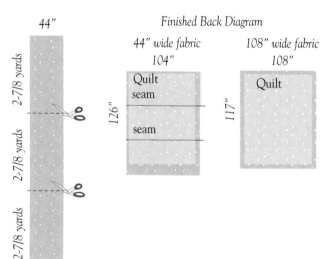

44"

2-7/8 yards

2-7/8 yards

2-7/8 yards

Finished Back Diagram

126"

44" wide fabric
104"

Quilt
seam

seam

117"

108" wide fabric
108"

Quilt

Quilting Suggestions:

- Pieced Blocks-**TB 8—11" Leaf Quartet**
- **BEIGE** alternate blocks-**TB 18—11" Lady Slipper**
- Side triangles-1/2 of **TB 18—11" Lady Slipper**
- Corner triangles-1/4 of **TB 18—11" Lady Slipper**
- Inner border-**TB 93—1-1/2" M-Border**
- Outer border-**TB 113—7-1/2" Floral Vine**

Binding
Cutting

From **RUST PRINT**:
- Cut 11, 2-3/4 x 44-inch strips

Sew binding to quilt using a 3/8-inch seam allowance. This measurement will produce a 1/2-inch wide finished double binding. Refer to **Binding and Diagonal Piecing** on page 140 for complete instructions.

Wedding Quilt
91 x 108-inches

Spring Fling Throw

66-inches square

Fabrics & Supplies

3/8 yard **ROSE PRINT**
for pinwheel units, lattice post squares

2-1/8 yards **BLUE/ROSE FLORAL**
for pinwheel units, lattice segments, outer border

1-2/3 yards **DARK BLUE PRINT**
for blocks, inner border, pieced border

1-5/8 yards **BEIGE PRINT** for blocks, pieced border

5/8 yard **GREEN PRINT** for blocks, corner squares

5/8 yard **DARK BLUE PRINT** for binding

4 yards for backing

quilt batting, at least 72-inches square

Before beginning this project, read through
Getting Started *on page 131.*

Blocks

Makes 9 blocks

Cutting

From **ROSE PRINT**:
• Cut 2, 3-7/8 x 44-inch strips

From **BLUE/ROSE FLORAL**:
• Cut 2, 3-7/8 x 44-inch strips

From **DARK BLUE PRINT**:
• Cut 8, 2 x 44-inch strips. From strips cut:
  144, 2-inch squares

From **BEIGE PRINT**:
• Cut 13, 2 x 44-inch strips. From strips cut:
  144, 2 x 3-1/2-inch rectangles

From **GREEN PRINT**:
• Cut 4, 3-1/2 x 44-inch strips. From strips cut:
  36, 3-1/2-inch squares

Piecing

Note: *Refer to arrows on diagrams for pressing.*

Step 1 With right sides together, layer 3-7/8 x 44-inch **BLUE/ROSE FLORAL** and **ROSE** strips together in pairs. Press together, but do not sew. Cut the layered strips into squares. Cut the layered squares in half diagonally to make 36 sets of triangles. Stitch 1/4-inch from the diagonal edge of each pair of triangles; press.

Crosscut 18,
3-7/8-inch squares

Make 36, 3-1/2-inch
triangle-pieced squares

Step 2 Sew the triangle-pieced squares together in pairs; press. Sew the pairs together to make the pinwheel units; press. At this point each block should measure 6-1/2-inches square.

Make 18

Make 9

Step 3 With right sides together, position a 2-inch **DARK BLUE** square on the left corner of a 2 x 3-1/2-inch **BEIGE** rectangle. Draw a diagonal line on the square; stitch on the line. Trim the seam allowance to 1/4-inch; press. Make 144 units. Sew 4 units together; press. Make (36) 4-piece units. At this point each 4-piece unit should measure 3-1/2 x 6-1/2-inches.

Make 144

Make 36 units

Step 4 Sew Step 3 units to the top/bottom edges of the pinwheel units; press. Sew 3-1/2-inch **GREEN** squares to the remaining Step 3 units; press. Sew the units to the side edges of the pinwheel units; press. At this point each block should measure 12-1/2-inches square.

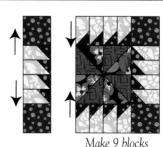

Make 9 blocks

Quilt Center

Cutting

From **BLUE/ROSE FLORAL**:
- Cut 4, 4-1/2 x 44-inch strips. From strips cut: 12, 4-1/2 x 12-1/2-inch lattice segments

From **ROSE PRINT**:
- Cut 1, 4-1/2 x 44-inch strip. From strip cut: 4, 4-1/2-inch lattice post squares

Quilt Center Assembly

Note: *Refer to arrows on diagrams for pressing.*

Step 1   Sew together (3) pieced blocks and (2) 4-1/2 x 12-1/2-inch **BLUE/ROSE FLORAL** lattice segments; press. At this point each block row should measure 12-1/2 x 44-1/2-inches.

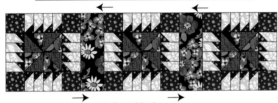

Make 3 block rows

Step 2   Sew together (3) 4-1/2 x 12-1/2-inch **BLUE/ROSE FLORAL** lattice segments and (2) 4-1/2-inch **ROSE** lattice post squares; press. At this point each lattice strip should measure 4-1/2 x 44-1/2-inches.

Make 2 lattice strips

Step 3   Referring to the quilt diagram on page 83, sew together the block rows and the lattice strips; press. At this point the quilt center should measure 44-1/2-inches square.

Borders

Note: *Yardage given allows for border strips to be cut on the crosswise grain. Diagonally piece strips as needed, referring to* **Diagonal Piecing** *instructions on page 140. Read through* **Border** *instructions on page 139 for general instructions on adding borders.*

Cutting

From **DARK BLUE PRINT**:
- Cut 6, 4-1/2 x 44-inch strips. From strips cut: 24, 4-1/2 x 8-1/2-inch rectangles

- Cut 5, 2-1/2 x 44-inch inner border strips

From **BEIGE PRINT**:
- Cut 6, 4-1/2 x 44-inch strips. From strips cut: 48, 4-1/2-inch squares

From **GREEN PRINT**:
- Cut 4, 4-1/2-inch corner squares

From **BLUE/ROSE FLORAL**:
- Cut 7 to 8, 5-1/2 x 44-inch outer border strips

Assembling and Attaching the Borders

Step 1   Attach 2-1/2-inch wide **DARK BLUE** inner border strips.

Step 2   With right sides together, position a 4-1/2-inch **BEIGE** square on the corner of a 4-1/2 x 8-1/2-inch **DARK BLUE** rectangle. Draw a diagonal line on the square; stitch on the line, trim, and press. Repeat this process at the opposite corner of the rectangle.

Make 12

Make 12

Step 3   Sew the Step 2 units together in pairs. Press seam allowances open. At this point each unit should measure 4-1/2 x 16-1/2-inches.

Make 12

Step 4   Sew (3) Step 3 units together for each pieced border. Press seam allowances open. At this point each pieced border strip should measure 4-1/2 x 48-1/2-inches.

Make 4 pieced borders

Step 5   Sew pieced border strips to the top/bottom edges of the quilt center; press. Sew 4-1/2-inch **GREEN** corner squares to both ends of the remaining pieced border strips; press. Sew the pieced border strips to the side edges of the quilt center; press.

Step 6   Attach 5-1/2-inch wide **BLUE/ROSE FLORAL** outer border strips.

Putting It All Together

Cut the 4 yard length of backing fabric in half crosswise to make 2, 2 yard lengths. Refer to **Finishing the Quilt** on page 140 for complete instructions. Our project was quilted with an all over quilt design.

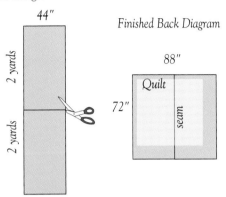

Finished Back Diagram

Binding

Cutting

From **DARK BLUE PRINT**:
- Cut 7, 2-3/4 x 44-inch strips

Sew binding to quilt using a 3/8-inch seam allowance. This measurement will produce a 1/2-inch wide finished double binding. Refer to **Binding and Diagonal Piecing** on page 140 for complete instructions.

Spring Fling
66-inches square

Summer Surpise Quilt

64 x 86-inches

Fabrics & Supplies

1 yard **GREEN DOT** for blocks

1 yard **BEIGE PRINT** for blocks

1 yard **GOLD PRINT** for blocks

1-1/4 yards **GREEN PRINT** for blocks,
vertical lattice strips, middle border

1-1/2 yards **ROSE PRINT** for lattice segments,
vertical lattice strips, inner border

1-7/8 yards **GREEN/BEIGE/ROSE FLORAL**
for outer border

3/4 yard **GREEN PRINT** for binding

5-1/4 yards for backing

quilt batting, at least 70 x 92-inches

Before beginning this project, read through
Getting Started *on page 131.*

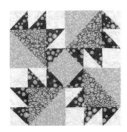

Blocks

Makes 15 blocks

Cutting

From **GREEN DOT**:
- Cut 10, 2-7/8 x 44-inch strips

From **BEIGE PRINT**:
- Cut 7, 2-7/8 x 44-inch strips

- Cut 4, 2-1/2 x 44-inch strips. From strips cut:
  60, 2-1/2-inch squares

From **GOLD PRINT**:
- Cut 4, 4-7/8 x 44-inch strips

- Cut 3, 2-7/8 x 44-inch strips

From **GREEN PRINT**:
- Cut 4, 4-7/8 x 44-inch strips

Piecing

Note: Refer to arrows on diagrams for pressing.

Step 1   With right sides together, layer (7) 2-7/8 x 44-inch **GREEN DOT** strips and the 2-7/8 x 44-inch **BEIGE** strips in pairs. Press together, but do not sew. Cut the layered strips into squares. Cut the layered squares in half diagonally to make 180 sets of triangles. Stitch 1/4-inch from the diagonal edge of each pair of triangles; press.

Crosscut 90,
2-7/8-inch squares   *Make 180, 2-1/2-inch*
triangle-pieced squares

Step 2   With right sides together, layer (3) 2-7/8 x 44-inch **GREEN DOT** strips and the 2-7/8 x 44-inch **GOLD** strips in pairs. Press together, but do not sew. Cut the layered strips into squares. Cut the layered squares in half diagonally to make 60 sets of triangles. Stitch 1/4-inch from the diagonal edge of each pair of triangles; press.

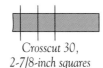

Crosscut 30,
2-7/8-inch squares   *Make 60, 2-1/2-inch*
triangle-pieced squares

Step 3   With right sides together, layer the 4-7/8 x 44-inch **GOLD** and **GREEN PRINT** strips in pairs. Press together, but do not sew. Cut the layered strips into squares. Cut the layered squares in half diagonally to make 60 sets of triangles. Stitch 1/4-inch from the diagonal edge of each pair of triangles; press.

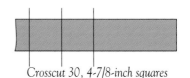

Crosscut 30, 4-7/8-inch squares

Make 60, 4-1/2-inch
triangle-pieced squares

Step 4 Sew the Step 1 triangle-pieced squares together in pairs. Make 60 units. Sew the pairs to the top edge of each of the Step 3 triangle-pieced squares; press. <u>At this point each unit should measure 4-1/2 x 6-1/2-inches.</u>

Make 60

Make 60

Step 5 Sew together the remaining Step 1 and Step 2 triangle-pieced squares in pairs; press. Make 60 units. Sew a 2-1/2-inch **BEIGE** square to the left edge of each unit; press. <u>At this point each unit should measure 2-1/2 x 6-1/2-inches.</u> Sew the units to the right edge of each Step 4 unit; press. <u>At this point each unit should measure 6-1/2-inches square.</u>

Make 60

Make 60

Step 6 Sew the Step 5 units together in pairs; press. Sew the pairs together; press. <u>At this point each block should measure 12-1/2-inches square.</u>

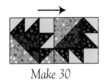

Make 30

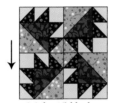

Make 15 blocks

Quilt Center

Note: *Yardage given allows for lattice strips to be cut on crosswise grain. Diagonally piece strips as needed referring to* **Diagonal Piecing** *instructions on page 140.*

Cutting

From **ROSE PRINT**:
- Cut 4, 2-1/2 x 44-inch strips. From strips cut: 12, 2-1/2 x 12-1/2-inch lattice segments
- Cut 8 more 2-1/2 x 44-inch strips for vertical lattice strips

From **GREEN PRINT**:
- Cut 4, 1-1/2 x 44-inch vertical lattice strips

Quilt Center Assembly

Step 1 Sew together (5) pieced blocks and (4) 2-1/2 x 12-1/2-inch **ROSE** lattice segments; press. <u>At this point each block row should measure 12-1/2 x 68-1/2-inches.</u>

Step 2 From the 1-1/2-inch wide **GREEN PRINT** strip cut 2 vertical lattice strips 68-1/2-inches long (or to the measurement of your block rows).

Step 3 From the 2-1/2-inch wide **ROSE** strip cut 4 vertical lattice strips 68-1/2-inches long (or to the measurement of your block rows).

Step 4 Aligning long edges, sew 2-1/2-inch wide **ROSE** lattice strips to both side edges of a 1-1/2-inch wide **GREEN PRINT** lattice strip. Press seam allowances toward the **GREEN PRINT** strip. Make 2 vertical lattice strips.

Step 5 Referring to the quilt diagram, sew together the block rows and the vertical lattice strips. Press seam allowances toward the vertical lattice strips.

Make 3 block rows

Borders

Note: Yardage given allows for border strips to be cut on crosswise grain. Diagonally piece strips as needed referring to **Diagonal Piecing** *instructions on page 140. Read through* **Border** *instructions on page 139 for general instructions on adding borders.*

Cutting

From **ROSE PRINT**:
- Cut 7, 2-1/2 x 44-inch inner border strips

From **GREEN PRINT**:
- Cut 7, 1-1/2 x 44-inch middle border strips

From **GREEN/BEIGE/ROSE FLORAL**:
- Cut 9, 6-1/2 x 44-inch outer border strips

Attaching the Borders

Step 1   Attach 2-1/2-inch wide **ROSE** inner border strips.

Step 2   Attach 1-1/2-inch wide **GREEN PRINT** middle border strips.

Step 3   Attach 6-1/2-inch wide **GREEN/BEIGE/ROSE FLORAL** outer border strips.

Putting It All Together

Cut the 5-1/4 yard length of backing fabric in half crosswise to make 2, 2-5/8 yard lengths. Refer to **Finishing the Quilt** on page 140 for complete instructions. Our project was quilted with an all over quilt design.

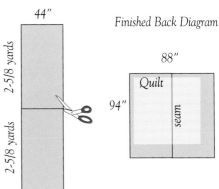

44"

2-5/8 yards

2-5/8 yards

Finished Back Diagram

88"

94"   Quilt

seam

Binding

Cutting

From **GREEN PRINT**:
- Cut 8, 2-3/4 x 44-inch strips

Sew binding to quilt using a 3/8-inch seam allowance. This measurement will produce a 1/2-inch wide finished double binding. Refer to **Binding and Diagonal Piecing** on page 140 for complete instructions.

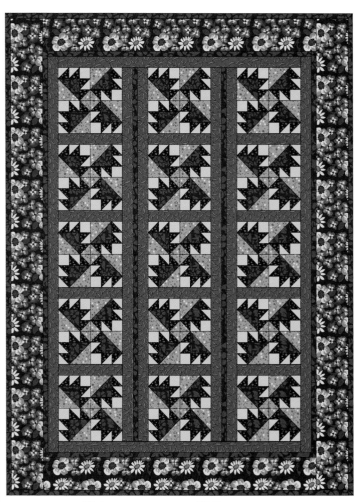

Summer Surprise
64 x 86-inches

Calendar Sampler

Lynette introduced the Block of the
Month concept to quilters more than
20 years ago and Thimbleberries® Block of the
Month patterns have led the way ever since.

Calendar Sampler Throw

72 x 89-inches

Calendar Sampler Throw

Fabrics & Supplies for the 12 Blocks

January Block

1/8 yard BEIGE PRINT
1/8 yard PURPLE PRINT
1/4 yard BLUE PRINT
1/8 yard GOLD PRINT
1/8 yard GREEN PRINT

February Block

1/4 yard GOLD PRINT
1/4 yard BEIGE PRINT
1/4 yard MEDIUM BLUE FLORAL
1/4 yard RED FLORAL
1/8 yard GREEN PRINT
1/8 yard CHESTNUT PRINT
1/8 yard DARK BLUE PRINT
1/8 yard RED PRINT
3-inch square BLACK
for appliqué birdhouse hole

March Block

1/4 yard GREEN PRINT
1/4 yard GOLD FLORAL
1/8 yard TERRA-COTTA PRINT
1/8 yard BRICK PRINT
1/8 yard BEIGE PRINT

April Block

1/4 yard GOLD PRINT
1/8 yard PLUM PRINT
1/8 yard LIGHT GREEN PRINT
1/8 yard BEIGE PRINT
1/8 yard DARK GREEN PRINT

May Block

1/4 yard PURPLE PRINT
1/4 yard GOLD PRINT
1/4 yard ROSE PRINT
1/8 yard GREEN PRINT #1
1/8 yard GREEN PRINT #2
1/8 yard DARK GREEN PRINT #3
1/4 yard BEIGE PRINT

June Block

1/8 yard GREEN PRINT
1/8 yard ROSE PRINT
1/8 yard PURPLE PRINT
1/8 yard GOLD PRINT
1/8 yard BEIGE PRINT

July Block

1/4 yard GOLD PRINT
1/8 yard BLUE PRINT
1/8 yard RED PRINT
1/8 yard BEIGE PRINT

August Block

1/8 yard GREEN PRINT
1/4 yard PEACH PRINT
1/4 yard ORANGE PRINT
1/4 yard BEIGE PRINT

September Block

1/8 yard GOLD PRINT
1/8 yard MEDIUM GREEN PRINT
1/8 yard RED PRINT
1/8 yard DARK GREEN PRINT
1/8 yard BROWN PRINT
1/4 yard BEIGE PRINT

October Block

1/4 yard CORAL PRINT
1/8 yard ORANGE DIAGONAL PRINT
1/8 yard DARK ORANGE PRINT
1/8 yard GREEN PRINT
1/8 yard BEIGE PRINT

November Block

1/4 yard RUST PRINT
1/8 yard BEIGE PRINT
1/8 yard RUST FLORAL
1/8 yard LIGHT GOLD PRINT
1/8 yard GREEN PRINT
1/8 yard GOLD/RUST PRINT

December Block

1/4 yard GREEN PRINT
1/8 yard RED PRINT
1/4 yard BEIGE PRINT

Fabrics & Supplies for Finishing the Quilt

3-3/8 yards BEIGE FLORAL for lattice posts/segments, inner border, outer border

1-1/2 yards BROWN PRINT for block borders, lattice posts, first middle border

1 yard GREEN PRINT for lattice segments, second middle border

3/4 yard BEIGE FLORAL for binding

5-1/4 yards for backing

paper-backed fusible web

quilt batting, at least 78 x 95-inches

Before beginning this project, read through **Getting Started** *on page 131.*

January Block

Cutting

From **BEIGE PRINT**:
- Cut 1, 2-7/8 x 44-inch strip.
  From strip cut:
  6, 2-7/8-inch squares
  8, 2-1/2-inch squares

From **PURPLE PRINT**:
- Cut 4, 2-1/2-inch squares

From **BLUE PRINT**:
- Cut 1, 4-1/2-inch square

- Cut 4, 2-7/8-inch squares

From **GOLD PRINT**:
- Cut 1, 2-7/8 x 44-inch strip. From strip cut:
  6, 2-7/8-inch squares
  4, 2-1/2 x 4-1/2-inch rectangles

From **GREEN PRINT**:
- Cut 1, 2-1/2 x 44-inch strip. From strip cut:
  4, 2-1/2 x 4-1/2-inch rectangles
  8, 2-1/2-inch squares

Piecing

Note: *Refer to arrows on diagrams for pressing.*

Step 1 With right sides together, position a 2-1/2-inch **PURPLE** square on 2 opposite corners of the 4-1/2-inch **BLUE** square. Draw a diagonal line on the small squares; stitch on the lines, trim, and press. Repeat this process at the remaining corners of the large square. <u>At this point the unit should measure 4-1/2-inches square.</u>

Make 1

Step 2 With right sides together, position a 2-1/2-inch **GREEN** square on the corner of a 2-1/2 x 4-1/2-inch **GOLD** rectangle. Draw a diagonal line on the square; stitch on the line, trim, and press. Repeat this process at the opposite corner of the rectangle.

Make 4

Step 3 With right sides together, layer (4) 2-7/8-inch **GOLD** and **BEIGE** squares in pairs. Press together, but do not sew. Cut the layered squares in half diagonally to make 8 sets of triangles. Stitch 1/4-inch from the diagonal edge of each pair of triangles; press.

Make 8, 2-1/2-inch triangle-pieced squares

Step 4 With right sides together, position a Step 3 triangle-pieced square on the corner of a 2-1/2 x 4-1/2-inch **GREEN** rectangle (note the angle of the seam line). Draw a diagonal line on the triangle-pieced square; stitch on the line, trim, and press. Repeat this process at the opposite corner of the rectangle. <u>At this point each unit should measure 2-1/2 x 4-1/2-inches.</u>

Make 4

Step 5 Sew the Step 2 and Step 4 units together in pairs; press. Sew (2) units to the top/bottom edges of the Step 1 unit; press. <u>At this point the unit should measure 4-1/2 x 12-1/2-inches.</u>

Step 8 Sew the Step 6 and Step 7 units together in pairs; press. Sew the units to the top/bottom edges of the remaining Step 5 units; press. <u>At this point each unit should measure 4-1/2 x 12-1/2-inches.</u>

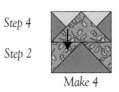

Step 4

Step 2

Make 4

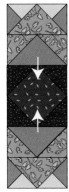

Make 1

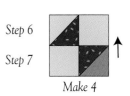

Step 6

Step 7

Make 4

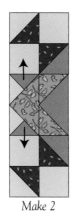

Make 2

Step 6 With right sides together, layer together (2) 2-7/8-inch **BLUE** and **BEIGE** squares in pairs. Press together, but do not sew. Cut the layered squares in half diagonally to make 4 sets of triangles. Stitch 1/4-inch from the diagonal edge of each pair of triangles; press. Sew a 2-1/2-inch **BEIGE** square to the right edge of the triangle-pieced squares; press. <u>At this point each unit should measure 2-1/2 x 4-1/2-inches.</u>

Step 9 Sew together the Step 5 and Step 8 units; press. <u>At this point the block should measure 12-1/2-inches square.</u>

Make 4, 2-1/2-inch triangle-pieced squares   *Make 4*

Make 1

Step 7 With right sides together, layer (2) 2-7/8-inch **BLUE** and **GOLD** squares in pairs. Press together, but do not sew. Cut the layered squares in half diagonally to make 4 sets of layered triangles. Stitch 1/4-inch from the diagonal edge of each pair of triangles; press. Sew a 2-1/2-inch **BEIGE** square to the left edge of the triangle-pieced squares; press. <u>At this point each unit should measure 2-1/2 x 4-1/2-inches.</u>

Make 4, 2-1/2-inch triangle-pieced squares   *Make 4*

February Block

Cutting

From **GOLD PRINT**:
- Cut 1, 4-1/2 x 44-inch strip.
  From strip cut:
  1, 4-1/2 x 8-1/2-inch rectangle
  2, 4-1/2-inch squares
  4, 1-1/2-inch squares

From **BEIGE PRINT**:
- Cut 2, 4-1/2-inch squares

From **MEDIUM BLUE FLORAL**:
- Cut 1, 4-1/2 x 8-1/2-inch rectangle

From **RED FLORAL**:
- Cut 1, 7-1/2 x 8-1/2-inch rectangle
- Cut 2, 1-1/2 x 4-1/2-inch rectangles

From **GREEN PRINT**:
- Cut 1, 2-1/2 x 4-1/2-inch rectangle

From **CHESTNUT PRINT**:
- Cut 1, 2-1/2 x 4-1/2-inch rectangle

From **DARK BLUE PRINT**:
- Cut 1, 2-1/2 x 4-1/2-inch rectangle

From **RED PRINT**:
- Cut 1, 2-1/2 x 4-1/2-inch rectangle

From **BLACK**:
- Cut 1, 3-inch square for appliqué birdhouse hole

Piecing

Note: *Refer to arrows on diagrams for pressing.*

Step 1 With right sides together, position a 4-1/2-inch **BEIGE** square on the left corner of the 4-1/2 x 8-1/2-inch 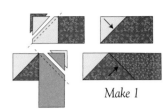 **GOLD** rectangle. Draw a diagonal line on the square; stitch on the line, trim, and press. Position the 4-1/2 x 8-1/2-inch **MEDIUM BLUE** rectangle on the right corner of the rectangle. Draw a diagonal line on the **MEDIUM BLUE** rectangle; stitch on the line, trim, and press.

Make 1

Step 2 With right sides together, position a 4-1/2-inch **BEIGE** square on the right corner of the Step 1 unit. Draw a diagonal line on the square; stitch on the line, trim, and press. At this point the roof unit should measure 4-1/2 x 12-1/2-inches.

Make 1

Step 3 With right sides together, position a 4-1/2-inch **GOLD** square on the lower left corner of the 7-1/2 x 8-1/2-inch **RED FLORAL** rectangle. Draw a diagonal line on the square; stitch on the line, trim, and press. Repeat this process at the adjacent corner of the rectangle.

7-1/2"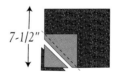

Make 1

Step 4 With right sides together, position 1-1/2-inch **GOLD** squares on the corners of a 1-1/2 x 4-1/2-inch **RED FLORAL** rectangle. Draw a diagonal line on the squares; stitch on the lines, trim, and press. Make 2 units. Sew the units together; press. Sew this unit to the top edge of the Step 3 unit; press. At this point the heart unit should measure 8-1/2-inches square.

Make 2

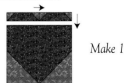

Make 1

Step 5 Sew together the 2-1/2 x 4-1/2-inch **GREEN, CHESTNUT, DARK BLUE,** and **RED PRINT** rectangles; press. <u>At this point the unit should measure 4-1/2 x 8-1/2-inches.</u>

Make 1

Step 6 Sew the heart unit to the left edge of the Step 5 unit; press. Sew the roof unit to the top edge of this unit; press. <u>At this point the house unit should measure 12-1/2-inches square.</u>

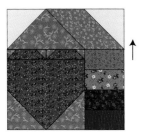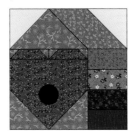

Make 1

Appliqué the Birdhouse Hole Fusible Web Method

Step 1 Trace the circle onto the paper side of the fusible web.

Step 2 Following the manufacturer's instructions, fuse the shape to the wrong side of the black fabric square. Let the fabric cool and cut along the traced line. Peel away the paper backing from the fusible web.

Step 3 Position the circle shape on the block; fuse in place. Machine zigzag stitch around the shape using black thread. You could hand blanket stitch around the shape with pearl cotton.

Birdhouse Hole
Template

BLACK

March Block

Cutting

From **GREEN PRINT**:
- Cut 2, 4-7/8-inch squares
- Cut 4, 2-1/2-inch squares

From **GOLD FLORAL**:
- Cut 2, 4-7/8-inch squares

From **TERRA-COTTA PRINT**:
- Cut 1, 2-1/2 x 21-inch strip. From strip cut: 8, 2-1/2-inch squares

From **BRICK PRINT**:
- Cut 1, 2-1/2 x 20-inch strip. From strip cut: 4, 2-1/2 x 4-1/2-inch rectangles

From **BEIGE PRINT**:
- Cut 1, 2-1/2 x 44-inch strip. From strip cut: 8, 2-1/2 x 4-1/2-inch rectangles

Piecing

Note: *Refer to arrows on diagrams for pressing.*

Step 1 With right sides together, layer the 4-7/8-inch **GOLD FLORAL** and **GREEN** squares in pairs. Press together, but do not sew. Cut the layered squares in half diagonally to make 4 sets of triangles. Stitch 1/4-inch from the diagonal edge of each pair of triangles; press.

Make 4, 4-1/2-inch triangle-pieced squares

Step 2 With right sides together, position a 2-1/2-inch **TERRA-COTTA** square on the **GREEN** corner of a Step 1 triangle-pieced square. Draw a diagonal line on the square; stitch on the line, trim, and press. Repeat this process on the **GOLD FLORAL** corner of the triangle-pieced square. At this point each unit should measure 4-1/2-inches square. Sew the units together in pairs; press. Sew the pairs together to make a square which should measure 8-1/2-inches square.

   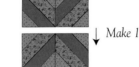

Make 4

↓ *Make 1*

Step 3 With right sides together, position a 2-1/2 x 4-1/2-inch **BEIGE** rectangle on the corner of a 2-1/2 x 4-1/2-inch **BRICK** rectangle. Draw a diagonal line on the **BEIGE** rectangle; stitch on the line, trim, and press. Repeat this process at the opposite corner of the **BRICK** rectangle. At this point each unit should measure 2-1/2 x 8-1/2-inches.

Make 4

Step 4 Sew Step 3 units to the sides of the Step 2 square; press. At this point the unit should measure 8-1/2 x 12-1/2-inches.

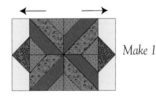

Make 1

Step 5 Sew 2-1/2-inch **GREEN** squares to both ends of the remaining Step 3 units; press. At this point each unit should measure 2-1/2 x 12-1/2-inches.

Make 2

Step 6 Sew the units together; press. At this point the block should measure 12-1/2-inches square.

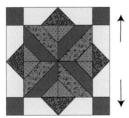

Make 1

April Block

Cutting

From **GOLD PRINT**:
- Cut 1, 2-1/2-inch square
- Cut 2, 1-1/2 x 44-inch strips.
  From strips cut:
  8, 1-1/2 x 3-1/2-inch rectangles
  16, 1-1/2-inch squares

From **PLUM PRINT**:
- Cut 2, 1-1/2 x 44-inch strips. From strips cut:
  2, 1-1/2 x 6-1/2-inch rectangles
  2, 1-1/2 x 4-1/2-inch rectangles
  8, 1-1/2 x 3-1/2-inch rectangles
  4, 1-1/2-inch squares

From **LIGHT GREEN PRINT**:
- Cut 1, 1-1/2 x 44-inch strip. From strip cut:
  2, 1-1/2 x 4-1/2-inch rectangles
  2, 1-1/2 x 2-1/2-inch rectangles

From **BEIGE PRINT**:
- Cut 2, 1-1/2 x 44-inch strips. From strips cut:
  4, 1-1/2 x 6-1/2-inch rectangles
  8, 1-1/2 x 2-1/2-inch rectangles
  20, 1-1/2-inch squares

From **DARK GREEN PRINT**:
- Cut 1, 2-1/2 x 44-inch strip. From strip cut:
  4, 2-1/2-inch squares
  16, 1-1/2-inch squares

Piecing

Note: *Refer to arrows on diagrams for pressing.*

Step 1   Sew 1-1/2 x 2-1/2-inch **LIGHT GREEN** rectangles to the top/bottom edges of the 2-1/2-inch **GOLD** square; press.

Make 1

Step 2   With right sides together, position 1-1/2-inch **PLUM** squares on the corners of a 1-1/2 x 4-1/2-inch **LIGHT GREEN** rectangle. Draw a diagonal line on the squares; stitch on the lines, trim, and press. Sew the units to both side edges of the Step 1 unit; press. <u>At this point the unit should measure 4-1/2-inches square.</u>

Make 2

Make 1

Step 3   Sew the 1-1/2 x 4-1/2-inch **PLUM** rectangles to the top/bottom edges of the Step 2 unit and sew the 1-1/2 x 6-1/2-inch **PLUM** rectangles to the side edges; press. <u>At this point the unit should measure 6-1/2-inches square.</u>

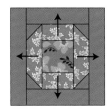

Make 1

Step 4   With right sides together, position 1-1/2-inch **GOLD** squares on the corners of a 1-1/2 x 3-1/2-inch **PLUM** rectangle. Draw a diagonal line on the squares; stitch on the lines, trim, and press. Make 8 units. Repeat this process using 1-1/2-inch **BEIGE** squares and 1-1/2 x 3-1/2-inch **GOLD** rectangles. Make 8 units. <u>At this point each unit should measure 1-1/2 x 3-1/2-inches.</u>

Make 8

Make 8

Step 5   Sew the Step 4 units together in pairs; press. Sew the pairs together; press. Sew a 1-1/2 x 6-1/2-inch **BEIGE** rectangle to the top edge of the units; press.

Make 8

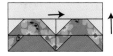

Make 4

Step 6   Sew the Step 5 units to the side edges of the Step 3 unit; press. <u>At this point the unit should measure 6-1/2 x 12-1/2-inches.</u>

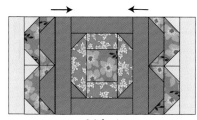

Make 1

Step 7   With right sides together, position a 1-1/2-inch **DARK GREEN** square on the corner of a 1-1/2 x 2-1/2-inch **BEIGE** rectangle. Draw a diagonal line on the square; stitch on the line, trim, and press. Repeat this process at the opposite corner of the rectangle. Sew the units to the top edge of the 2-1/2-inch **DARK GREEN** squares; press. Sew a 1-1/2-inch **BEIGE** square to each of the remaining units; press. Sew the units together; press. <u>At this point each unit should measure 3-1/2-inches square.</u>

Make 8

Make 4

Step 8   Sew the Step 7 units to both edges of the remaining Step 5 units; press. Sew the units to the top/bottom edges of the Step 6 unit; press. <u>At this point the block should measure 12-1/2-inches square.</u>

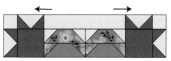

Make 2

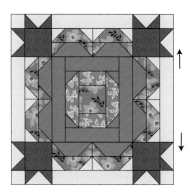

Make 1

May Block

Cutting

From **PURPLE**, **GOLD**,
and **ROSE PRINTS**:

- Cut 1, 5-1/4-inch square from each fabric.
  Cut the squares diagonally into quarters.
  You will be using only 1 triangle from
  each fabric.

- Cut 1, 4-7/8-inch square from each fabric.
  Cut the squares in half diagonally. You will
  be using only 1 triangle from each fabric.

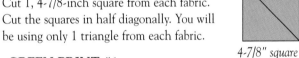

5-1/4" square

4-7/8" square

From **GREEN PRINT #1**:

- Cut 2, 2 x 7-inch rectangles

- Cut 2, 2 x 4-1/2-inch rectangles

From **GREEN PRINT #2**:

- Cut 2, 2 x 7-inch rectangles

From **DARK GREEN PRINT**:

- Cut 2, 1-1/2 x 8-1/2-inch rectangles

- Cut 1, 1-1/2 x 4-1/2-inch rectangle

From **BEIGE PRINT**:

- Cut 1, 5-1/4 x 44-inch strip.
  From strip cut:
  1, 5-1/4-inch square. Cut the square
  diagonally into quarters. You will be using
  only 3 of the triangles.

5-1/4" square

- Cut 1, 4-1/2-inch square
  4, 2 x 3-1/2-inch rectangles
  6, 2-inch squares

Piecing

Note: *Refer to arrows on diagrams for pressing.*

Step 1   With right sides together, sew the **BEIGE** triangles to each of the **PURPLE**, **GOLD**, and **ROSE** triangles; press. Sew a corresponding color triangle to each of these units; press. <u>At this point each flower unit should measure 4-1/2-inches square.</u>

Bias edges

Make 1 flower unit from each fabric

Step 2   With right sides together, position a 2 x 3-1/2-inch **BEIGE** rectangle on the right corner of the 2 x 7-inch **GREEN #1** rectangle. Draw a diagonal line on the **BEIGE** rectangle; stitch on the line, trim, and press. Repeat this process at the left corner of the **GREEN** rectangle using a 2-inch **BEIGE** square.

Make 1

Step 3   Repeat Step 2 using a 2 x 7-inch **GREEN #2** rectangle. Notice the placement of the **BEIGE** rectangle and the direction of the stitching lines.

Make 1

Step 4   Sew the Step 2 and Step 3 leaves to both side edges of a 1-1/2 x 8-1/2-inch **DARK GREEN** rectangle; press. Sew the **ROSE** flower unit to the top edge of the leaf unit; press. <u>At this point the **ROSE** flower unit should measure 4-1/2 x 12-1/2-inches.</u>

Make 1

Step 5 Make the **PURPLE** flower unit in the same manner. With right sides together, position a 2 x 3-1/2-inch **BEIGE** rectangle on the right corner of the 2 x 7-inch **GREEN #2** rectangle. Draw a diagonal line on the **BEIGE** rectangle; stitch on the line, trim, and press. Repeat this process at the left corner of the **GREEN** rectangle using a 2-inch **BEIGE** square.

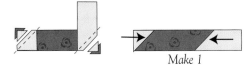

Make 1

Step 6 Repeat Step 5 using a 2 x 7-inch **GREEN #1** rectangle. Notice the placement of the **BEIGE** rectangle and the direction of the stitching lines.

Make 1

Step 7 Sew the Step 5 and Step 6 leaves to both side edges of a 1-1/2 x 8-1/2-inch **DARK GREEN** rectangle; press. Sew the **PURPLE** flower unit to the top edge of the leaf unit; press. At this point the **PURPLE** flower unit should measure 4-1/2 x 12-1/2-inches.

Make 1

Step 8 With right sides together, position a 2-inch **BEIGE** square on the corner of the 2 x 4-1/2-inch **GREEN #1** rectangle. Draw a diagonal line on the square; stitch on the line, trim, and press. Repeat this process for the remaining 2 x 4-1/2-inch **GREEN #1** rectangle, notice the direction of the stitching line. Sew the leaf units to both side edges of a 1-1/2 x 4-1/2-inch **DARK GREEN** rectangle; press. Sew the **GOLD** flower unit and the

4-1/2-inch **BEIGE** square to the top edge of the leaf unit; press. At this point the **GOLD** flower unit should measure 4-1/2 x 12-1/2-inches.

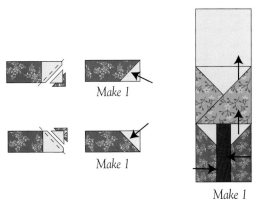

Make 1

Make 1

Make 1

Step 9 Sew together the **ROSE**, **GOLD**, and **PURPLE** tulips; press. At this point the block should measure 12-1/2-inches square.

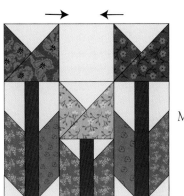

Make 1

June Block

Cutting

From **GREEN PRINT**:
- Cut 1, 2-1/2 x 44-inch strip.
  From strip cut:
  4, 2-1/2 x 3-1/2-inch rectangles
  4, 2-1/2 -inch squares
  8, 1-1/2-inch squares

From **ROSE PRINT**:
- Cut 4, 2-1/2-inch squares

From **PURPLE PRINT**:
- Cut 1, 2-1/2 x 44-inch strip. From strip cut:
  8, 2-1/2 x 3-1/2-inch rectangles
  8, 1-1/2-inch squares

From **GOLD PRINT**:
- Cut 5, 2-1/2-inch squares

From **BEIGE PRINT**:
- Cut 1, 1-1/2 x 44-inch strip. From strip cut:
  8, 1-1/2-inch squares
  4, 1-1/2 x 3-1/2-inch rectangles
  4, 1-1/2 x 2-1/2-inch rectangles

- Cut 1, 2-1/2 x 44-inch strip. From strip cut:
  8, 2-1/2-inch squares

Piecing

Note: *Refer to arrows on diagrams for pressing.*

Step 1 With right sides together, position a 1-1/2-inch
GREEN square on the corner of a 2-1/2-inch
ROSE square. Draw a diagonal line on the

small square; stitch on the line, trim, and press.
Repeat this process at the adjacent corner of
the **ROSE** square.

   Make 4

Step 2 With right sides together, position 1-1/2-inch
PURPLE squares on opposite corners of a
2-1/2-inch **GREEN** square. Draw diagonal
lines on the small squares; stitch on the lines,
trim, and press.

  Make 4

Step 3 Sew Step 1 units to the top/bottom edges of a
2-1/2-inch **GOLD** square; press. Sew Step 2 units to
the top/bottom edges of the remaining Step 1 units;
press. Sew the units together; press. <u>At this point
the unit should measure 6-1/2-inches square.</u>

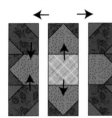 *Make 1*

Step 4 With right sides together, position a 1-1/2-inch
BEIGE square on the corner of a 2-1/2 x 3-1/2-inch
GREEN rectangle. Draw a diagonal line on the
square; stitch on the line, trim, and press. Repeat
this process at the adjacent corner of the rectangle.

   Make 4

Step 5 With right sides together, position a 2-1/2-inch
BEIGE square on the right corner of a
2-1/2 x 3-1/2-inch **PURPLE** rectangle. Draw a
diagonal line on the square; stitch on the line,
trim, and press. Repeat this process with the
remaining **PURPLE** rectangles, note the change
in the direction of the drawn lines.

  Make 4   *Make 4*

Step 6 Sew the Step 5 units to both side edges of the Step 4 units; press. <u>At this point each unit should measure 3-1/2 x 6-1/2-inches.</u> Sew 2 units to the top/bottom edges of the Step 3 unit; press. <u>At this point each unit should measure 6-1/2 x 12-1/2-inches.</u>

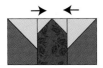

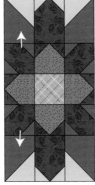

Make 4

Make 1

Step 7 Sew a 1-1/2 x 2-1/2-inch **BEIGE** rectangle to the top edge of a 2-1/2-inch **GOLD** square and sew a 1-1/2 x 3-1/2-inch **BEIGE** rectangle to the left edge; press. <u>At this point each unit should measure 3-1/2-inches square.</u>

   Make 4

Step 8 Sew the Step 7 units to the top/bottom edges of the remaining Step 6 units; press. Sew the 3 units together; press. <u>At this point the block should measure 12-1/2-inches square.</u>

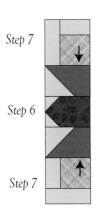

Step 7

Step 6

Step 7

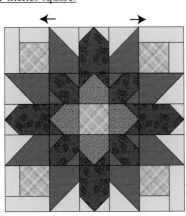

Make 1

July Block

Cutting

From **GOLD PRINT**:
- Cut 1, 4-1/2 x 44-inch strip.
  From strip cut:
  1, 4-1/2-inch square
  8, 2-1/2-inch squares

From **BLUE PRINT**:
- Cut 1, 2-1/2 x 44-inch strip. From strip cut:
  8, 2-1/2-inch squares
  4, 2-1/2 x 4-1/2-inch rectangles

From **RED PRINT**:
- Cut 1, 2-1/2 x 44-inch strip. From strip cut:
  3, 2-1/2 x 13-inch strips

From **BEIGE PRINT**:
- Cut 1, 1-1/2 x 44-inch strip. From strip cut:
  2, 1-1/2 x 13-inch strips

Piecing

Note: *Refer to arrows on diagrams for pressing.*

Step 1 With right sides together, position a 2-1/2-inch **GOLD** square on the corner of a 2-1/2 x 4-1/2-inch **BLUE** rectangle. Draw a diagonal line on the square; stitch on the line, trim, and press. Repeat this process at the opposite corner of the rectangle to make star point units.

Make 4 star point units

Step 2 Sew star point units to the top/bottom edges of the 4-1/2-inch **GOLD** square; press. Sew 2-1/2-inch **BLUE** squares to both edges of the remaining star point units; press. Sew the units to the side edges of the square; press. <u>At this point the star square should measure 8-1/2-inches square.</u>

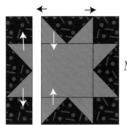

Make 1

Step 3 Aligning long edges, sew together the 1-1/2 x 13-inch **BEIGE** strips and the 2-1/2 x 13-inch **RED** strips; press. Cut the strip set into segments to make pieced border units.

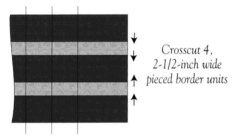

Crosscut 4, 2-1/2-inch wide pieced border units

Step 4 Sew pieced border units to the top/bottom edges of the star block; press. Sew 2-1/2-inch **BLUE** squares to both edges of the remaining border units; press. Sew the pieced border units to the side edges of the star block; press. <u>At this point the block should measure 12-1/2-inches square.</u>

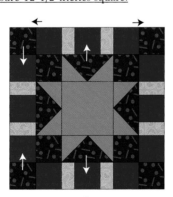

Make 1

August Block
Cutting

From **GREEN PRINT**:
- Cut 4, 2-1/2-inch squares
- Cut 1, 1-1/2 x 7-inch strip for stem unit

From **PEACH PRINT**:
- Cut 1, 4-1/2-inch square
- Cut 3, 2-1/2-inch squares

From **ORANGE PRINT**:
- Cut 1, 2-1/2 x 44-inch strip. From strip cut: 16, 2-1/2-inch squares
- Cut 3, 2-7/8-inch squares

From **BEIGE PRINT**:
- Cut 1, 4-1/4-inch square for stem unit
- Cut 1, 2-7/8 x 38-inch strip. From strip cut: 3, 2-7/8-inch squares
- Cut 1, 2-1/2 x 44-inch strip. From strip cut: 8, 2-1/2 x 4-1/2-inch rectangles 3, 2-1/2-inch squares

Piecing

Note: Refer to arrows on diagrams for pressing.

Step 1 With right sides together, position 2-1/2-inch **GREEN** squares on opposite corners of the 4-1/2-inch **PEACH** square. Draw a diagonal line on the small squares; stitch on the lines, trim, and press. Repeat this process at the remaining corners of the **PEACH** square. At this point the unit should measure 4-1/2-inches square.

Make 1

Step 2 With right sides together, position a 2-1/2-inch **ORANGE** square on the corner of a 2-1/2 x 4-1/2-inch **BEIGE** rectangle. Draw a diagonal line on the square; stitch on the line, trim, and press. Repeat this process at the opposite corner of the rectangle.

Make 8

Step 3 Sew the Step 2 units together in pairs; press. Sew 2 units to the top/bottom edges of the Step 1 unit; press.

Make 4

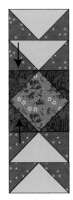

Make 1

Step 4 With right sides together, layer the 2-7/8-inch **ORANGE** and **BEIGE** squares in pairs. Press together, but do not sew. Cut the layered squares in

half diagonally to make 6 sets of triangles. Stitch 1/4-inch from the diagonal edge of each pair of triangles; press.

Make 6, 2-1/2-inch triangle-pieced squares

Step 5 Sew a 2-1/2-inch **PEACH** square to the left edge of 3 triangle-pieced squares; press. Sew a 2-1/2-inch **BEIGE** square to the right edge of the remaining 3 triangle-pieced squares; press. Sew the units together in pairs; press. At this point each unit should measure 4-1/2-inches square.

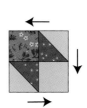

Make 3

Step 6 To make the stem unit, cut the 4-1/4-inch **BEIGE** square in half diagonally to make 2 triangles. Center a triangle on the 1-1/2 x 7-inch **GREEN** strip; stitch together with a 1/4-inch seam allowance. Press seam allowance toward the **GREEN** strip. Center the remaining triangle on the opposite edge of the **GREEN** strip; stitch and press. Trim stem unit so it measures 4-1/2-inches square.

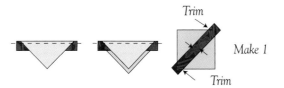

Trim

Make 1

Trim

Step 7 Sew the units together in 3 vertical rows; press. Sew the rows together; press. At this point the block should measure 12-1/2-inches square.

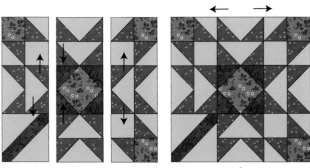

Make 1

September Block

Cutting

From **GOLD, MEDIUM GREEN,** and
RED PRINTS for apples:
- Cut 1, 4 x 44-inch strip from *each* fabric.
  From *each* strip cut:
  2, 4 x 4-1/2-inch rectangles
  4, 1 x 2-inch rectangles

From **DARK GREEN PRINT**:
- Cut 1, 2-7/8 x 44-inch strip. From strip cut:
  3, 2-7/8-inch squares
  6, 2 x 2-1/2-inch rectangles
  6, 1-inch squares

From **BROWN PRINT**:
- Cut 1, 1 x 44-inch strip. From strip cut:
  6, 1 x 2-inch rectangles
  6, 1-inch squares

From **BEIGE PRINT**:
- Cut 1, 2-7/8 x 44-inch strip. From strip cut:
  3, 2-7/8-inch squares
  6, 2-inch squares
  12, 1-inch squares

- Cut 1, 1-1/2 x 44-inch strip. From strip cut:
  12, 1-1/2-inch squares
  18, 1 x 1-1/2-inch rectangles

Piecing

Note: *Refer to arrows on diagrams for pressing.*

Step 1   With right sides together, position 1-1/2-inch **BEIGE** squares on the lower corners of a 4 x 4-1/2-inch **GOLD** rectangle. Draw a diagonal line on the squares; stitch on the lines, trim, and press. Position 1-inch **BEIGE** squares on the upper corners of the rectangle. Draw a diagonal line on the squares; stitch on the lines, trim, and press. Make 2 apple units using the **MEDIUM GREEN** and **RED** apple fabrics.

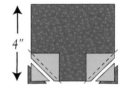 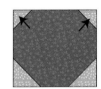

*Make 2 using each
apple fabric*

Step 2   With right sides together, position a 1 x 1-1/2-inch **BEIGE** rectangle on the left corner of a 1 x 2-inch **GOLD** rectangle. Draw a diagonal line on the **BEIGE** rectangle; stitch on the line, trim, and press. Position a 1-inch **BROWN** square on the right corner of the **GOLD** rectangle. Draw a diagonal line on the square; stitch on the line, trim, and press. At this point each unit should measure 1 x 2-1/2-inches.

*Make 2 of
each color*

Step 3   With right sides together, position a 1 x 1-1/2-inch **BEIGE** rectangle on the corner of a 1 x 2-inch **GOLD** rectangle. Draw a diagonal line on the **BEIGE** rectangle; stitch on the line, trim, and press. At this point each unit should measure 1 x 2-1/2-inches.

*Make 2 of
each color*

Step 4   Sew the Step 2 and 3 units together in pairs; press. Sew these units to the top edge of the corresponding Step 1 units; press. <u>At this point each apple unit should measure 4-1/2-inches square.</u>

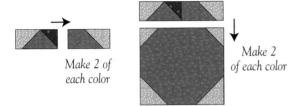

Make 2 of each color   *Make 2 of each color*

Step 5   With right sides together, position a 2-inch **BEIGE** square on the corner of a 2 x 2-1/2-inch **DARK GREEN** rectangle. Draw a diagonal line on the square; stitch on the line, trim, and press.

Make 6

Step 6   With right sides together, position a 1-inch **GREEN** square on the left corner of a 1 x 2-inch **BROWN** rectangle. Draw a diagonal line on the square; stitch on the line, trim, and press. Position a 1 x 1-1/2-inch **BEIGE** rectangle on the right corner of the **BROWN** rectangle. Draw a diagonal line on the rectangle; stitch on the line, trim, and press. Sew the stem unit to the right edge of the Step 5 leaf unit; press. <u>At this point each leaf/stem unit should measure 2-1/2-inches square.</u>

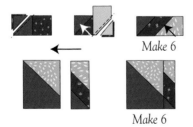

Make 6

Make 6

Step 7   With right sides together, layer the 2-7/8-inch **BEIGE** and **GREEN** squares together in pairs. Press together, but do not sew. Cut each square in half diagonally to make 6 sets of layered triangles. Stitch 1/4-inch from the diagonal edge

of each pair of triangles; press. Sew the leaf/stem units to the left edge of each of the triangle-pieced squares; press. <u>At this point each leaf unit should measure 2-1/2 x 4-1/2-inches.</u>

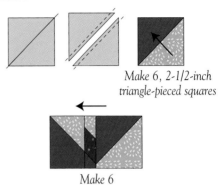

Make 6, 2-1/2-inch triangle-pieced squares

Make 6

Step 8   Sew the leaf units to the top edge of the apple units; press. Sew the apple blocks together; press. <u>At this point the block should measure 12-1/2-inches square.</u>

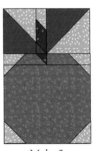

Make 2 of each color

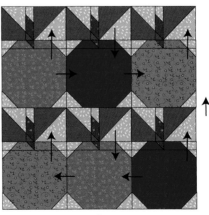

Make 1

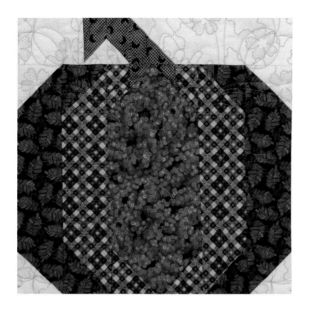

October Block

Cutting

From **CORAL PRINT**:
- Cut 1, 4-1/2 x 9-1/2-inch rectangle
- Cut 1, 1-1/2 x 2-1/2-inch rectangle

From **ORANGE DIAGONAL PRINT**:
- Cut 1, 2-1/2 x 44-inch strip. From strip cut:
  2, 2-1/2 x 10-1/2-inch rectangles
  2, 2-1/2-inch squares
  4, 1-1/2-inch squares

From **DARK ORANGE PRINT**:
- Cut 1, 2-1/2 x 44-inch strip. From strip cut:
  2, 2-1/2 x 10-1/2-inch rectangles
  4, 2-1/2-inch squares

From **GREEN PRINT**:
- Cut 1, 2-1/2-inch square
- Cut 2, 1-1/2 x 2-1/2-inch rectangles
- Cut 2, 1-1/2-inch squares

From **BEIGE PRINT**:
- Cut 1, 2-1/2 x 44-inch strip. From strip cut:
  1, 2-1/2 x 7-1/2-inch rectangle
  1, 2-1/2 x 3-1/2-inch rectangle
  4, 2-1/2-inch squares
  2, 1-1/2-inch squares

Piecing

Note: *Refer to arrows on diagrams for pressing.*

Step 1   With right sides together, position 2-1/2-inch **BEIGE** squares on the corners of a 2-1/2 x 10-1/2-inch **DARK ORANGE** rectangle. Draw a diagonal line on the squares; stitch on the lines, trim, and press.

Make 2

Step 2   With right sides together, position 2-1/2-inch **DARK ORANGE** squares on the corners of a 2-1/2 x 10-1/2-inch **ORANGE DIAGONAL** rectangle. Draw a diagonal line on the squares; stitch on the lines, trim, and press.

Make 2

Step 3   With right sides together, position a 2-1/2-inch **ORANGE DIAGONAL** square on the upper left corner of the 4-1/2 x 9-1/2-inch **CORAL** rectangle. Draw a diagonal line on the square; stitch on the line, trim, and press. Position a 1-1/2-inch **ORANGE DIAGONAL** square on the upper right corner of the rectangle. Draw a diagonal line on the square; stitch, trim, and press. Repeat this process using a 2-1/2-inch **ORANGE DIAGONAL** square on the lower left corner and using a 1-1/2-inch **ORANGE DIAGONAL** square on the lower right corner of the rectangle. At this point the pumpkin center should measure 4-1/2 x 9-1/2-inches.

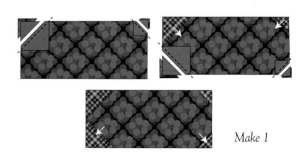

Make 1

Step 4 With right sides together, position a 1-1/2-inch **GREEN** square on the corner of the 1-1/2 x 2-1/2-inch **CORAL** rectangle. Draw a diagonal line on the square; stitch on the line, trim, and press. Repeat this process at the opposite corner of the rectangle. Sew 1-1/2-inch **ORANGE DIAGONAL** squares to both ends of the unit; press. Sew this unit to top edge of the Step 3 unit; press. At this point the pumpkin center should measure 4-1/2 x 10-1/2-inches.

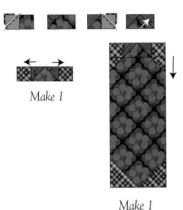

Make 1

Step 5 Sew together the Step 1, 2, and 4 units; press. At this point the pumpkin unit should measure 10-1/2 x 12-1/2-inches.

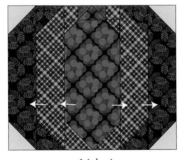

Make 1

Step 6 With right sides together, position a 1-1/2-inch **BEIGE** square on the corner of the 1-1/2 x 2-1/2-inch **GREEN** rectangle. Draw a diagonal line on the square; stitch on the line, trim, and press. Make 1 unit. Repeat this process, note the change in direction of the stitching line. Make 1 unit. Sew the units together and sew the 2-1/2 x 3-1/2-inch **BEIGE** rectangle to the left edge of the unit; press.

Make 1   *Make 1*   *Make 1*

Step 7 With right sides together, position a 2-1/2-inch **GREEN** square on the corner of the 2-1/2 x 7-1/2-inch **BEIGE** rectangle. Draw a diagonal line on the square; stitch on the line, trim, and press. Sew the Step 6 unit to the left edge of the unit; press. At this point the stem unit should measure 2-1/2 x 12-1/2-inches.

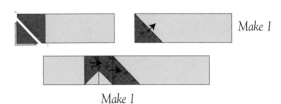

Make 1

Make 1

Step 8 Sew the stem unit to top edge of the pumpkin unit; press. At this point the block should measure 12-1/2-inches square.

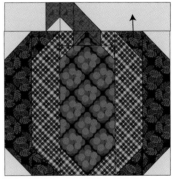

Make 1

November Block

Cutting

From RUST PRINT:
- Cut 1, 4-1/2-inch square
- Cut 4, 1-1/2 x 3-1/2-inch rectangles
- Cut 4, 1-1/2 x 2-1/2-inch rectangles

From BEIGE PRINT:
- Cut 1, 2-1/2 x 44-inch strip. From strip cut: 12, 2-1/2-inch squares
- Cut 1, 1-1/2 x 44-inch strip. From strip cut: 16, 1-1/2-inch squares

From RUST FLORAL:
- Cut 1, 2-1/2 x 44-inch strip. From strip cut: 8, 2-1/2 x 4-1/2-inch rectangles

From LIGHT GOLD PRINT:
- Cut 8, 2-1/2-inch squares

From GREEN PRINT:
- Cut 1, 1-1/2 x 44-inch strip. From strip cut:
  4, 1-1/2 x 4-1/2-inch rectangles
  4, 1-1/2 x 3-1/2-inch rectangles

From GOLD/RUST PRINT:
- Cut 4, 2-1/2-inch squares

Piecing

Note: *Refer to arrows on diagrams for pressing.*

Step 1 With right sides together, position 2-1/2-inch **BEIGE** squares on opposite corners of a 4-1/2-inch **RUST** square. Draw diagonal lines on the small squares; stitch on the lines, trim, and press. Repeat this process at the remaining corners of the large square. <u>At this point the unit should measure 4-1/2-inches square.</u>

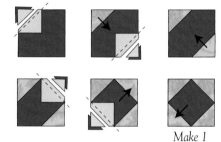

Make 1

Step 2 With right sides together, position a 2-1/2-inch **LIGHT GOLD** square on the corner of a 2-1/2 x 4-1/2-inch **RUST FLORAL** rectangle. Draw a diagonal line on the square; stitch on the line, trim, and press. Repeat this process at the opposite corner of the rectangle.

Make 4

Step 3 With right sides together, position a 2-1/2-inch **BEIGE** square on the corner of a 2-1/2 x 4-1/2-inch **RUST FLORAL** rectangle. Draw a diagonal line on the square; stitch on the line, trim, and press. Repeat this process at the opposite corner of the rectangle. Sew a Step 2 unit to the bottom edge of each of these units; press. <u>At this point each unit should measure 4-1/2-inches square.</u>

Make 4

Make 4

Step 4 Sew Step 3 units to the side edges of the Step 1 unit; press. At this point the unit should measure 4-1/2 x 12-1/2-inches.

Make 1

Step 5 With right sides together, position a 1-1/2-inch **BEIGE** square on the corner of a 1-1/2 x 2-1/2-inch **RUST** rectangle. Draw a diagonal line on the square; stitch on the line, trim, and press. Make 4 A units. Repeat this process with a 1-1/2-inch **BEIGE** square and a 1-1/2 x 3-1/2-inch **RUST** rectangle. Notice the direction of the drawn line. Make 4 B units.

Make 4
A Unit

Make 4
B Unit

Step 6 Sew A units to the bottom edge of the 2-1/2-inch **GOLD/RUST FLORAL** squares and sew B units to the right edge; press.

B

A

Make 4

Step 7 With right sides together, position a 1-1/2-inch **BEIGE** square on the corner of a 1-1/2 x 3-1/2-inch **GREEN** rectangle. Draw a diagonal line on the square; stitch on the line, trim, and press. Make 4 A units. Repeat this process with a 1-1/2-inch **BEIGE** square and a 1-1/2 x 4-1/2-inch **GREEN** rectangle. Notice the direction of the drawn line. Make 4 B units.

Make 4
A Unit

Make 4
B Unit

Step 8 Sew A units to the bottom edge of the Step 6 units and sew B units to the right edge; press. At this point each unit should measure 4-1/2-inches square.

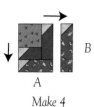

B

A

Make 4

Step 9 Sew Step 8 units to the side edges of the remaining Step 3 units; press. At this point each unit should measure 4-1/2 x 12-1/2-inches.

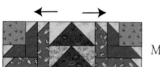

Make 2

Step 10 Sew the units together; press. At this point the block should measure 12-1/2-inches square.

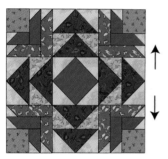

Make 1

December Block

Cutting

From **GREEN PRINT**:
- Cut 1, 4-1/2 x 44-inch strip. From strip cut:
  1, 4-1/2 x 8-1/2-inch rectangle
  1, 4-1/2 x 12-1/2-inch rectangle
  1, 2-1/2 x 12-1/2-inch rectangle

From **RED PRINT**:
- Cut 1, 2-1/2 x 8-1/2-inch rectangle

From **BEIGE PRINT**:
- Cut 1, 4-1/2 x 44-inch strip. From strip cut:
  2, 4-1/2 x 6-1/2-inch rectangles
  2, 4-1/2-inch squares
  2, 2-1/2-inch squares
  2, 2-1/2 x 4-1/2-inch rectangles

Piecing

Note: *Refer to arrows on diagrams for pressing.*

Step 1 With right sides together, position a 4-1/2 x 6-1/2-inch **BEIGE** rectangle on the corner of the 4-1/2 x 8-1/2-inch **GREEN** rectangle. Draw a diagonal line on the **BEIGE** rectangle; stitch on the line, trim, and press. Repeat this process on the opposite corner of the **GREEN** rectangle. At this point the unit should measure 4-1/2 x 12-1/2-inches.

Make 1

Step 2 With right sides together, position 4-1/2-inch **BEIGE** squares on the corners of the 4-1/2 x 12-1/2-inch **GREEN** rectangle. Draw a diagonal line on the squares; stitch on the lines, trim, and press. At this point the unit should measure 4-1/2 x 12-1/2-inches.

Make 1

Step 3 With right sides together, position 2-1/2-inch **BEIGE** squares on the corners of the 2-1/2 x 12-1/2-inch **GREEN** rectangle. Draw a diagonal line on the squares; stitch on the lines, trim, and press. At this point the unit should measure 2-1/2 x 12-1/2-inches.

Make 1

Step 4 With right sides together, position 2-1/2 x 4-1/2-inch **BEIGE** rectangles on the corners of the 2-1/2 x 8-1/2-inch **RED** rectangle. Draw a diagonal line on the **BEIGE** rectangles; stitch on the lines, trim, and press. At this point the unit should measure 2-1/2 x 12-1/2-inches.

Make 1

Step 5 Sew the units together; press. At this point the block should measure 12-1/2-inches square.

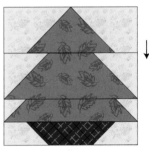

Make 1

Quilt Center

Quilt Center and Lattice Strips

Cutting

From **BROWN PRINT**:

- Cut 22, 1-1/2 x 44-inch strips for block borders

- Cut 2, 1-1/2 x 44-inch strips. From strips cut:
  3, 1-1/2 x 20-inch strips for lattice post squares

From **BEIGE FLORAL**:

- Cut 18, 1-1/2 x 44-inch strips for lattice segments

- Cut 2, 1-1/2 x 44-inch strips. From strips cut:
  3, 1-1/2 x 20-inch strips for lattice post squares

From **GREEN PRINT**:

- Cut 9, 1-1/2 x 44-inch strips for lattice segments

Piecing

Note: *Refer to arrows on diagrams for pressing.*

Step 1 Referring to **Border** instructions on page 139, attach 1-1/2-inch wide **BROWN** strips to each of the 12 pieced blocks; press. At this point each block should measure 14-1/2-inches square.

Border all 12 Blocks

Step 2 With right sides together and long edges aligned, sew 1-1/2 x 20-inch **BEIGE FLORAL** strips to the side edges of a 1-1/2 x 20-inch **BROWN** strip. Press referring to *Hints and Helps for Pressing Strip Sets*. Cut the strip set into segments.

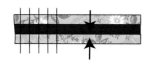

Crosscut 6, 1-1/2-inch wide segments

Hints and Helps for Pressing Strip Sets

When sewing strips of fabric together for strip sets, it is important to press the seam allowances nice and flat, usually to the dark fabric. Be careful not to stretch as you press, causing a "rainbow effect." This will affect the accuracy and shape of the pieces cut from the strip set. Press on the wrong side first with the strips perpendicular to the ironing board. Flip the piece over and press on the right side to prevent little pleats from forming at the seams. Laying the strip set lengthwise on the ironing board seems to encourage the rainbow effect.

Avoid this "rainbow effect"

Step 3 With right sides together and long edges aligned, sew 1-1/2 x 20-inch **BROWN** strips to the side edges of a 1-1/2 x 20-inch **BEIGE FLORAL** strip; press. Cut the strip set into segments.

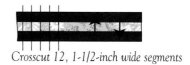

Crosscut 12, 1-1/2-inch wide segments

Step 4 Sew Step 3 segments to the side edges of the Step 2 segments to make 6 lattice post squares; press. At this point each lattice post square should measure 3-1/2-inches square.

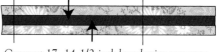

Make 6 lattice post squares

Step 5 With right sides together and long edges aligned, sew a 1-1/2 x 44-inch **BEIGE FLORAL** strip to the side edges of a 1-1/2 x 44-inch **GREEN** strip; press. Make 9 strip sets. Cut the strip sets into lattice segments.

Crosscut 17, 14-1/2-inch long lattice segments

Step 6 Referring to the quilt diagram on page 113 for block placement, sew together (3) pieced blocks and (2) 3-1/2 x 14-1/2-inch pieced lattice segments. Press seam allowances toward the lattice segments. Make 4 block rows. At this point each block row should measure 14-1/2 x 48-1/2-inches.

Step 7 Sew together (2) lattice post squares and (3) 3-1/2 x 14-1/2-inch pieced lattice segments; press. At this point each lattice strip should measure 3-1/2 x 48-1/2-inches.

Make 3 lattice segments

Step 8 Sew together the block rows and lattice strips; press. At this point the quilt center should measure 48-1/2 x 65-1/2-inches.

Borders

*Note: Yardage given allows for border strips to be cut on crosswise grain. Diagonally piece strips as needed referring to **Diagonal Piecing** instructions on page 140. Read through **Border** instructions on page 139 for general instructions on adding borders.*

Cutting

From **BEIGE FLORAL**:
- Cut 9, 8-1/2 x 44-inch outer border strips
- Cut 7, 1-1/2 x 44-inch inner border strips

From **BROWN PRINT**:
- Cut 7, 1-1/2 x 44-inch first middle border strips

From **GREEN PRINT**:
- Cut 7, 2-1/2 x 44-inch second middle border strips

Attaching the Borders

Step 1 Attach 1-1/2-inch wide **BEIGE FLORAL** inner border strips.

Step 2 Attach 1-1/2-inch wide **BROWN** first middle border strips.

Step 3 Attach 2-1/2-inch wide **GREEN** second middle border strips.

Step 4 Attach 8-1/2-inch wide **BEIGE FLORAL** outer border strips.

Putting It All Together

Cut the 5-1/4 yard length of backing fabric in half crosswise to make 2, 2-5/8 yard lengths. Refer to **Finishing the Quilt** on page 140 for complete instructions.

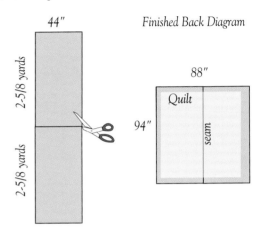

Finished Back Diagram

Quilting Suggestions:

- Pieced blocks-TB105—13-1/2" Bleeding Heart
- **GREEN/BEIGE** lattice segments TB115—2-1/2" Leaf Wave
- **BROWN/BEIGE** lattice post squares-in-the-ditch
- 3 narrow borders (quilt as 1 border) TB65—3-1/2" Nordic Scroll
- Outer border-TB109—7-1/2" Ivy Vine

Binding

Cutting

From **BEIGE FLORAL**:
- Cut 8 to 9, 2-3/4 x 44-inch strips

Sew binding to quilt using a 3/8-inch seam allowance. This measurement will produce a 1/2-inch wide finished double binding. Refer to **Binding and Diagonal Piecing** on page 140 for complete instructions.

Calendar Sampler Throw

72 x 89-inches

Apple Stand Table Runner

18 x 24-inches

Fabrics & Supplies

September Apple Block

1/8 yard **GOLD PRINT** for apples

1/8 yard **MEDIUM GREEN PRINT** for apples

1/8 yard **RED PRINT** for apples

1/8 yard **DARK GREEN PRINT** for leaves

1/8 yard **BROWN PRINT** for stems

1/4 yard **BEIGE PRINT** for background

Borders, Binding, Backing

1/4 yard **BEIGE PRINT**
for inner border, pieced border

1/4 yard **DARK GREEN PRINT** for pieced border

1/4 yard **GOLD FLORAL** for outer border

1/4 yard **GOLD FLORAL** for binding

2/3 yard for backing

quilt batting, at least 24 x 30-inches

Make the **SEPTEMBER APPLE BLOCK** *using the* **Cutting** *and* **Piecing** *instructions on pages 104 - 105. When the Apple Block is complete it should measure 12-1/2-inches square.*

Borders

Note: *Yardage given allows for border strips to be cut on crosswise grain. Read through* **Border** *instructions on page 139 for general instructions on adding borders.*

Cutting

From **BEIGE PRINT**:
- Cut 2, 1-1/2 x 44-inch inner border strips
- Cut 1, 1-1/2 x 44-inch strip. From strip cut: 28, 1-1/2-inch squares

From **DARK GREEN PRINT**:
- Cut 3, 1-1/2 x 44-inch strips. From strips cut: 28, 1-1/2 x 3-1/2-inch rectangles

From **GOLD FLORAL**:
- Cut 2, 2-1/2 x 44-inch outer border strips
- Cut 1, 1-1/2 x 44-inch strip. From strip cut: 28, 1-1/2-inch squares

Attaching Borders

Step 1   Attach 1-1/2-inch wide **BEIGE** inner border strips to the **APPLE BLOCK**; press.

Step 2   With right sides together, position a 1-1/2-inch **BEIGE** square on the corner of a 1-1/2 x 3-1/2-inch **DARK GREEN** rectangle. Draw a diagonal line on the square; stitch on the line. Trim seam allowance to 1/4-inch; press. Position a 1-1/2-inch **GOLD FLORAL** square on the opposite corner of the rectangle. Draw a diagonal line on the square; stitch on the line, trim, and press.

Make 28

Step 3   For the top/bottom pieced borders, sew together (14) Step 2 units; press. <u>At this point each pieced border should measure 3-1/2 x 14-1/2-inches.</u> Sew the pieced borders to the top/bottom edges of the quilt center; press.

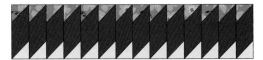

Make 2 pieced borders

Step 4   Attach 2-1/2-inch wide **GOLD FLORAL** outer border strips.

Putting It All Together

Trim batting and backing so they are 6-inches larger than the quilt top. Refer to **Finishing the Quilt** on page 140 for complete instructions.

Quilting Suggestions:

- **BEIGE** background-stipple
- Apples-circular design, in-the-ditch
- **GREEN** pieced border-in-the-ditch
- **GOLD FLORAL**-small meander

Binding

Cutting

From **GOLD FLORAL**:
- Cut 3, 2-3/4 x 44-inch strips

Sew binding to quilt using a 3/8-inch seam allowance. This measurement will produce a 1/2-inch wide finished double binding. Refer to **Binding and Diagonal Piecing** on page 140 for complete instructions.

Potholders

9-inches square

House Potholder

9-inches square

Fabrics & Supplies

3 x 21-inch piece **GOLD PRINT**

3 x 6-inch piece **BEIGE PRINT**

3 x 6-inch piece **MEDIUM BLUE PRINT**

5 x 10-inch piece **RED FLORAL**

3 x 4-inch piece **GREEN PRINT**

3 x 4-inch piece **CHESTNUT PRINT**

3 x 4-inch piece **DARK BLUE PRINT**

3 x 4-inch piece **RED PRINT**

2-inch square **BLACK PRINT**

1/8 yard **GOLD PRINT** for border

1/8 yard **GOLD PRINT** for binding

10-1/2-inch square for backing

10-1/2-inch square of **insulated batting** (Insul-Bright™)

1-1/2-inch square of paper-backed fusible web
for birdhouse hole

black pearl cotton or machine embroidery thread

basting spray (optional)

Cutting for Block

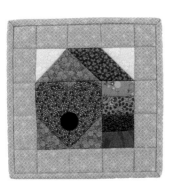

From **GOLD PRINT**:
- Cut 1,
2-1/2 x 4-1/2-inch rectangle

- Cut 2, 2-1/2-inch squares

- Cut 4, 1-inch squares

From **BEIGE PRINT**:
- Cut 2, 2-1/2-inch squares

From **MEDIUM BLUE PRINT**:
- Cut 1, 2-1/2 x 4-1/2-inch rectangle

From **RED FLORAL**:
- Cut 1, 4 x 4-1/2-inch rectangle

- Cut 2, 1 x 2-1/2-inch rectangles

From **GREEN PRINT**:
- Cut 1, 1-1/2 x 2-1/2-inch rectangle

From **CHESTNUT PRINT**:
- Cut 1, 1-1/2 x 2-1/2-inch rectangle

From **DARK BLUE PRINT**:
- Cut 1, 1-1/2 x 2-1/2-inch rectangle

From **RED PRINT**:
- Cut 1, 1-1/2 x 2-1/2-inch rectangle

From **BLACK**:
- Cut 1, 2-inch square for appliqué birdhouse hole

Piecing

Note: *Refer to arrows on diagrams for pressing.*

Step 1   With right sides together, position a 2-1/2-inch
BEIGE square on the left corner of the
2-1/2 x 4-1/2-inch **GOLD** rectangle. Draw a diagonal
line on the square; stitch on the line, trim, and press.
Position the 2-1/2 x 4-1/2-inch **MEDIUM BLUE**
rectangle on the right corner of the rectangle. Draw a
diagonal line on the **MEDIUM BLUE** rectangle;
stitch on the line, trim, and press.

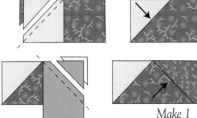

Make 1

Step 2 With right sides together, position a 2-1/2-inch **BEIGE** square on the right corner of the Step 1 unit. Draw a diagonal line on the square; stitch on the line, trim, and press. At this point the roof unit should measure 2-1/2 x 6-1/2-inches.

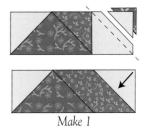

Make 1

Step 3 With right sides together, position a 2-1/2-inch **GOLD** square on the lower left corner of the 4 x 4-1/2-inch **RED FLORAL** rectangle. Draw a diagonal line on the square; stitch on the line, trim, and press. Repeat this process at the adjacent corner of the rectangle.

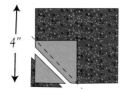

4"

Make 1

Step 4 With right sides together, position 1-inch **GOLD** squares on the corners of a 1 x 2-1/2-inch **RED FLORAL** rectangle. Draw a diagonal line on the squares; stitch on the lines, trim, and press. Make 2 units. Sew the units together; press. Sew this unit to the top edge of the Step 3 unit; press. At this point the heart unit should measure 4-1/2-inches square.

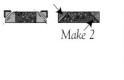

Make 2

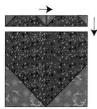

Make 1

Step 5 Sew together the 1-1/2 x 2-1/2-inch **GREEN, CHESTNUT, DARK BLUE,** and **RED** rectangles; press. At this point the unit should measure 2-1/2 x 4-1/2-inches.

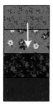

Make 1

Step 6 Sew the heart unit to the left edge of the Step 5 unit; press. Sew the roof unit to the top edge of this unit; press. At this point the house block should measure 6-1/2-inches square.

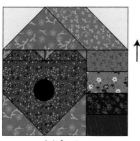

Make 1

Step 7 Prepare and attach the birdhouse hole referring to instructions on page 95.

Potholder Birdhouse Hole Template BLACK

POTHOLDER INSTRUCTIONS - Refer to *Potholder Instructions* on page 123 for general instructions on making the potholder.

Border
Cutting

From **GOLD PRINT**:
- Cut 1, 2 x 44-inch border strip

Sew border strip to block; press.

Binding
Cutting

From **GOLD PRINT**:
- Cut 1, 2-1/2 x 44-inch strip for binding

Sew binding to potholder using a 1/4-inch seam allowance. Refer to *Binding* on page 141 for complete instructions.

Star Potholder
9-inches square

Fabrics & Supplies

3 x 21-inch piece **GOLD PRINT**

4 x 21-inch piece **BLUE PRINT**

3 x 21-inch piece **RED PRINT**

3 x 21-inch piece **BEIGE PRINT**

1/8 yard **BROWN PRINT** for border

1/8 yard **BROWN PRINT** for binding

10-1/2-inch square for backing

10-1/2-inch square of **insulated batting** (Insul-Bright™)

basting spray (optional)

Cutting for Block

From **GOLD PRINT**:
- Cut 1, 2-1/2-inch square
- Cut 8, 1-1/2-inch squares

From **BLUE PRINT**:
- Cut 8, 1-1/2-inch squares
- Cut 4, 1-1/2 x 2-1/2-inch rectangles

From **RED PRINT**:
- Cut 3, 1-1/2 x 7-inch strips

From **BEIGE PRINT**:
- Cut 2, 1 x 7-inch strips

Piecing

Note: Refer to arrows on diagrams for pressing.

Step 1   With right sides together, position a 1-1/2-inch **GOLD** square on the corner of a 1-1/2 x 2-1/2-inch **BLUE** rectangle. Draw a diagonal line on the square; stitch on the line, trim, and press. Repeat this process at the opposite corner of the rectangle to make a star point unit.

Make 4 star point units

Step 2   Sew star point units to the top/bottom edges of the 2-1/2-inch **GOLD** square; press. Sew 1-1/2-inch **BLUE** squares to both edges of the remaining star point units; press. Sew the units to the side edges of the square; press. <u>At this point the star square should measure 4-1/2-inches square.</u>

Make 1

Step 3   Aligning long edges, sew together the 1 x 7-inch **BEIGE** strips and the 1-1/2 x 7-inch **RED** strips; press. Cut the strip set into segments to make the pieced border units. <u>At this point each pieced border should measure 1-1/2 x 4-1/2-inches.</u>

Crosscut 4, 1-1/2-inch wide segments for pieced border

Step 4   Sew pieced border units to the top/bottom edges of the star block; press. Sew 1-1/2-inch **BLUE** squares to both edges of the remaining pieced border units; press. Sew the border units to the side edges of the star block; press. <u>At this point the block should measure 6-1/2-inches square.</u>

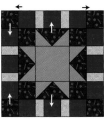

Make 1

POTHOLDER INSTRUCTIONS - Refer to **Potholder Instructions** on page 123 for general instructions on making the potholder.

Border
Cutting

From **BROWN PRINT**:
- Cut 1, 2 x 44-inch border strip

Sew border strip to block; press.

Binding
Cutting

From **BROWN PRINT**:
- Cut 1, 2-1/2 x 44-inch strip for binding

Sew binding to potholder using a 1/4-inch seam allowance. Refer to **Binding** on page 141 for complete instructions.

Pumpkin Potholder

9-inches square

Fabrics & Supplies

3 x 7-inch piece **CORAL PRINT**

3 x 20-inch piece **ORANGE DIAGONAL PRINT**

3 x 20-inch piece **DARK ORANGE PRINT**

3 x 10-inch piece **GREEN PRINT**

3 x 20-inch piece **BEIGE PRINT**

1/8 yard **BLACK PRINT** for border

1/8 yard **BLACK PRINT** for binding

10-1/2-inch square for backing

10-1/2-inch square of **insulated batting** (Insul-Bright™)

basting spray (optional)

Cutting for Block

From **CORAL PRINT**:
- Cut 1,
  2-1/2 x 5-inch rectangle

- Cut 1,
  1 x 1-1/2-inch rectangle

From **ORANGE DIAGONAL PRINT**:
- Cut 2, 1-1/2 x 5-1/2-inch rectangles

- Cut 2, 1-1/2-inch squares

- Cut 4, 1-inch squares

From **DARK ORANGE PRINT**:
- Cut 2, 1-1/2 x 5-1/2-inch rectangles

- Cut 4, 1-1/2-inch squares

From **GREEN PRINT**:
- Cut 1, 1-1/2-inch square

- Cut 2, 1 x 1-1/2-inch rectangles

- Cut 2, 1-inch squares

From **BEIGE PRINT**:
- Cut 1, 1-1/2 x 4-inch rectangle

- Cut 1, 1-1/2 x 2-inch rectangle

- Cut 4, 1-1/2-inch squares

- Cut 2, 1-inch squares

Piecing

Note: *Refer to arrows on diagrams for pressing.*

Step 1   With right sides together, position 1-1/2-inch **BEIGE** squares on the corners of a 1-1/2 x 5-1/2-inch **DARK ORANGE** rectangle. Draw a diagonal line on the squares; stitch on the lines, trim, and press.

Make 2

Step 2   With right sides together, position 1-1/2-inch **DARK ORANGE** squares on the corners of a 1-1/2 x 5-1/2-inch **ORANGE DIAGONAL** rectangle. Draw a diagonal line on the squares; stitch on the lines, trim, and press.

Make 2

Step 3   With right sides together, position a 1-1/2-inch **ORANGE DIAGONAL** square on the upper left corner of the 2-1/2 x 5-inch **CORAL** rectangle. Draw a diagonal line on the square; stitch on the line, trim, and press. Position a 1-inch **ORANGE DIAGONAL** square on the upper right corner of the rectangle. Draw a diagonal line on the square; stitch, trim, and press. Repeat this process using a 1-1/2-inch **ORANGE DIAGONAL** square on the lower left corner and using a 1-inch **ORANGE DIAGONAL** square on the lower right corner of the rectangle. At this point the pumpkin center should measure 2-1/2 x 5-inches.

Make 1

Step 4 With right sides together, position a 1-inch **GREEN** square on the corner of the 1 x 1-1/2-inch **CORAL** rectangle. Draw a diagonal line on the square; stitch on the line, trim, and press. Repeat this process at the opposite corner of the rectangle. Sew 1-inch **ORANGE DIAGONAL** squares to both ends of the unit; press. Sew this unit to top edge of the Step 3 unit; press. At this point the pumpkin center should measure 2-1/2 x 5-1/2-inches.

Make 1

Make 1

Step 5 Sew together the Step 1, 2, and 4 units; press. At this point the pumpkin unit should measure 5-1/2 x 6-1/2-inches.

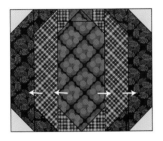

Make 1

Step 6 With right sides together, position a 1-inch **BEIGE** square on the corner of the 1 x 1-1/2-inch **GREEN** rectangle. Draw a diagonal line on the square; stitch on the line, trim, and press. Make 1 unit. Repeat this process, note the change in direction of the stitching line. Make 1 unit. Sew the units together and sew the 1-1/2 x 2-inch **BEIGE** rectangle to the left edge of the unit; press.

Make 1   Make 1   Make 1

Step 7 With right sides together, position a 1-1/2-inch **GREEN** square on the corner of the 1-1/2 x 4-inch **BEIGE** rectangle. Draw a diagonal line on the square; stitch on the line, trim, and press. Sew the Step 6 unit to the left edge of the unit; press. At this point the stem unit should measure 1-1/2 x 6-1/2-inches.

Make 1   Make 1

Step 8 Sew the stem unit to top edge of the pumpkin unit; press. At this point the block should measure 6-1/2-inches square.

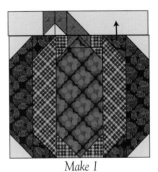

Make 1

POTHOLDER INSTRUCTIONS - Refer to *Potholder Instructions* on page 123 for general instructions on making the potholder.

Border

Cutting

From **BLACK PRINT**:
• Cut 1, 2 x 44-inch border strip

Sew border strip to block; press.

Binding

Cutting

From **BLACK PRINT**:
• Cut 1, 2-1/2 x 44-inch strip for binding

Sew binding to potholder using a 1/4-inch seam allowance. Refer to *Binding* on page 141 for complete instructions.

Tree Potholder

9-inches square

Fabrics & Supplies

3 x 20-inch piece **GREEN PRINT**

3 x 6-inch piece **RED PRINT**

3 x 20-inch piece **BEIGE PRINT**

1/8 yard **DARK GREEN PRINT** for border

1/8 yard **DARK GREEN PRINT** for binding

10-1/2-inch square for backing

10-1/2-inch square of **insulated batting** (Insul-Bright™)

basting spray (optional)

Cutting for Block

From **GREEN PRINT**:
- Cut 1,
  2-1/2 x 4-1/2-inch rectangle
- Cut 1,
  2-1/2 x 6-1/2-inch rectangle
- Cut 1,
  1-1/2 x 6-1/2-inch rectangle

From **RED PRINT**:
- Cut 1, 1-1/2 x 4-1/2-inch rectangle

From **BEIGE PRINT**:
- Cut 2, 2-1/2 x 3-1/2-inch rectangles
- Cut 2, 2-1/2-inch squares
- Cut 2, 1-1/2-inch squares
- Cut 2, 1-1/2 x 2-1/2-inch rectangles

Piecing

Note: *Refer to arrows on diagrams for pressing.*

Step 1   With right sides together, position a 2-1/2 x 3-1/2-inch **BEIGE** rectangle on the corner of the 2-1/2 x 4-1/2-inch **GREEN** rectangle. Draw a diagonal line on the **BEIGE** rectangle; stitch on the line, trim, and press. Repeat this process on the

opposite corner of the **GREEN** rectangle. <u>At this point the unit should measure 2-1/2 x 6-1/2-inches.</u>

Make 1   *Make 1*

Step 2   With right sides together, position 2-1/2-inch **BEIGE** squares on the corners of the 2-1/2 x 6-1/2-inch **GREEN** rectangle. Draw a diagonal line on the squares; stitch on the lines, trim, and press. <u>At this point the unit should measure 2-1/2 x 6-1/2-inches.</u>

Make 1

Step 3   With right sides together, position 1-1/2-inch **BEIGE** squares on the corners of the 1-1/2 x 6-1/2-inch **GREEN** rectangle. Draw a diagonal line on the squares; stitch on the lines, trim, and press. <u>At this point the unit should measure 1-1/2 x 6-1/2-inches.</u>

Make 1

Step 4   With right sides together, position 1-1/2 x 2-1/2-inch **BEIGE** rectangles on the corners of the 1-1/2 x 4-1/2-inch **RED** rectangle. Draw a diagonal line on the **BEIGE** rectangles; stitch on the lines, trim, and press. <u>At this point the unit should measure 1-1/2 x 6-1/2-inches.</u>

Make 1

Step 5   Sew the units together; press. <u>At this point the block should measure 6-1/2-inches square.</u>

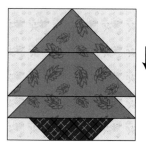

Make 1

POTHOLDER INSTRUCTIONS - Refer to *Potholder Instructions* for general instructions on making the potholder.

Border
Cutting

From **DARK GREEN PRINT**:
- Cut 1, 2 x 44-inch border strip

Sew border strip to block; press.

Binding
Cutting

From **DARK GREEN PRINT**:
- Cut 1, 2-1/2 x 44-inch strip for binding

Sew binding to potholder using a 1/4-inch seam allowance. Refer to **Binding** on page 141 for complete instructions.

Potholder Instructions

Step 1 Attach 2-inch wide **Border** strips referring to **Border** instructions on page 139. At this point the block should measure 9-1/2-inches square.

Step 2 With right sides facing out, layer the 9-1/2-inch **block** and the 10-1/2-inch **backing square** with the **insulated batting** sandwiched between the 2 layers. Hand baste or spray baste the layers together. Machine quilt the layered squares as desired.

Note: *If your layers shift as you sew, use a walking foot or lengthen your stitch length.*

Step 3 Trim the batting and backing even with the edges of the block. Zigzag stitch the edges to compress them and to hold them in place.

Step 4 Attach the 2-1/2-inch wide **Binding** strip referring to **Binding** instructions on page 141. Use a 1/4-inch seam allowance.

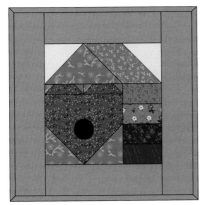

House Potholder

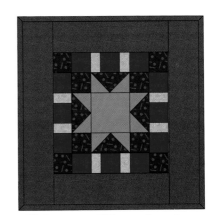

Star Potholder

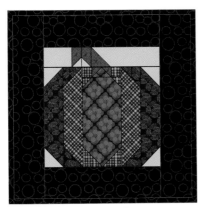

Pumpkin Potholder

Tree Potholder

City Tote

14" high x 9" wide x 3" deep

Fabrics & Supplies

7/8 yard **BLACK/GOLD PRINT** for front, back, large pocket, flap, small pocket/lining, straps

1/2 yard **BROWN DIAGONAL PRINT** for lining

2/3 yard **GOLD PRINT** for contrasting bottom, pocket lining/trim, inner pockets

1/2 yard **RED PRINT** for binding, button loop, strap trim

7/8 yard Fusible Fleece
(we used Pellon® Fusible Fleece)

(1) 3/4-inch diameter button

Before beginning this project, read through **Getting Started** *on page 131.*

Cutting

Note: Pocket Flap Pattern is on page 129.

From **BLACK/GOLD PRINT**:
- Cut 2, 13 x 15-inch rectangles for front/back
- Cut 3, 3 x 44-inch strips. Diagonal piece, cut: 2, 3 x 55-inch strips for straps
- Cut 1, 7-1/2 x 12-inch rectangle for small pocket/lining
- Cut 1, 7-1/2 x 7-3/4-inch rectangle for large pocket
- Cut 1, 5 x 8-inch rectangle for pocket flap

From **GOLD PRINT**:
- Cut 2, 13-1/2 x 14-1/2-inch rectangles for inner pockets
- Cut 1, 11 x 15-inch rectangle for contrasting bottom
- Cut 1, 7-1/2 x 8-3/4-inch rectangle for large pocket lining
- Cut 1, 5 x 8-inch rectangle pocket flap lining

From **BROWN DIAGONAL PRINT**:
- Cut 1, 13-1/2 x 31-1/2-inch rectangle for lining

From **RED PRINT**:
Note: Diagonally piece strips together as needed.

- Cut 3, 1 x 44-inch strips. From strips cut: 2, 55-inch long strips for strap trim
- Cut 1, 2-1/4 x 26-inch strip to bind top edge of tote
- Cut 1, 4-1/2-inch square for strap holder
- Cut 1, 1-1/2 x 3-inch strip for button loop
- Cut 1, 2-1/4 x 14-inch **bias** strip to bind pocket flap

From **FUSIBLE FLEECE**:
- Cut 2, 13 x 15-inch rectangles for tote front/back
- Cut 2, 1-1/4 x 55-inch strips for straps
- Cut 1, 11 x 15-inch rectangle for bottom
- Cut 1, 5 x 8-inch rectangle for pocket flap

Assembly

Step 1   Referring to Fusible Fleece manufacturer's instructions, prepare the front/back sections. Lay 13 x 15-inch Fusible Fleece rectangles on ironing board (fusible side up). Position 13 x 15-inch **BLACK/GOLD** rectangles on top of fleece (right side up). Cover with a press cloth; press to fuse. Machine quilt the front section layers and the back section layers. Our sample was quilted in a meandering fashion. Trim front and back sections to 11-1/4 x 13-1/2-inch rectangles.

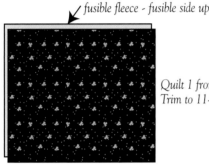

fusible fleece - fusible side up

*Quilt 1 front and 1 back
Trim to 11-1/4" x 13-1/2"*

Step 2   Lay 5 x 8-inch Fusible Fleece rectangle on ironing board (fusible side up). Position 5 x 8-inch **BLACK/GOLD** rectangle on top of fleece (right side up). Cover with a press cloth; press to fuse. Machine quilt the layers together. Using Pocket Flap Pattern on page 129, cut 1 quilted pocket flap and cut 1 pocket flap lining from the 5 x 8-inch **GOLD** rectangle. With wrong sides together, layer the **BLACK/GOLD** pocket flap on the **GOLD** lining, baste the raw edges together.

fusible fleece - fusible side up

Quilt pocket flap

Pocket flap

Step 3   Prepare button loop by folding in both long edges of the 1-1/2 x 3-inch **RED** strip so they meet in the middle, wrong sides together; press. Fold strip in half again; press and edge-stitch both long edges. At this point the button loop strip should be 3/8 x 3-inches. With raw edges aligned, center the button loop on

the **GOLD** side of the quilted pocket flap referring to page 129 for placement. Baste raw edges in place.

Pocket flap lining

Step 4   Prepare 2-1/4 x 14-inch **RED** *bias* binding strip referring to **Binding** instructions on page 141. Bind the curved edges of the **BLACK/GOLD** side of the pocket flap using a 1/4-inch seam allowance. Bring the binding to the **GOLD** lining side encasing the raw edges; hand stitch in place. The **RED** button loop will be hanging free.

raw edges

Step 5   With wrong sides together, fold 7-1/2 x 12-inch **BLACK/GOLD** rectangle in half crosswise to make a 7-1/2 x 6-inch rectangle for small pocket. Stitch a double edge-stitch at the top folded edge. Position the small pocket on the 7-1/2 x 7-3/4-inch **BLACK/GOLD** rectangle aligning side/bottom raw edges; baste together to make a large/small pocket unit.

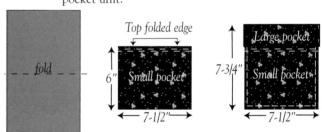

fold

Top folded edge

Small pocket

6"

7-1/2"

Large pocket

Small pocket

7-3/4"

7-1/2"

Step 6   Position the pocket flap at the top edge of the large/small pocket unit; baste in place. There should be 1/4-inch extra pocket fabric on both sides of the pocket flap for seam allowances.

1/4" extra   *1/4" extra*

Step 7 With right sides together, layer 7-1/2 x 8-3/4-inch **GOLD** lining rectangle on large/small pocket unit. Stitch lining and pocket unit together along the top edge of the large pocket. Bring the lining to the back of the pocket unit leaving 3/8-inch of the **GOLD** fabric showing at the top edge of the large pocket; press and stitch-in-the-ditch to secure the top **GOLD** trim. With raw edges aligned, baste in place. Stitch the button to the small pocket only.

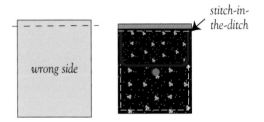

Step 8 Center pocket unit on the Step 1, 11-1/4 x 13-1/2-inch quilted front section with bottom edges aligned, baste in place.

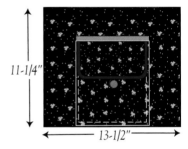

Step 9 To make straps, position a 1-1/4 x 55-inch Fusible Fleece strip down the center of the <u>wrong side</u> of a 3 x 55-inch **BLACK/GOLD** strip. Cover with a press cloth; press to fuse. Fold the long edges of the **BLACK/GOLD** strip over the fleece so they overlap in the middle, completely covering the fleece; press and baste down the center. <u>The strap should measure 1-1/4 x 55-inches.</u> Make 2 straps.

Step 10 To add strap trim, with wrong sides together, fold both long raw edges of a 1 x 55-inch **RED** strip in 1/4-inch toward the center of the strip; press. <u>At this point the strip should measure 1/2 x 55-inches.</u> Lay the **RED** strip on the prepared strap so that the raw edges of the strap are covered; pin. Edge-stitch along both long edges of the **RED** trim being sure to stitch in the same direction on each long edge to prevent puckering. Trim ends as needed. Repeat for second strap.

Step 11 Position a strap on the front section having bottom raw edges aligned. The strap needs to encase the side edges of the pocket unit; pin in place. Edge-stitch along both long edges of the strap being careful to keep the pocket flap free. Stitch in the same direction on both sides of the strap to prevent puckering. Stop stitching 2-inches from the top edge of the front section. Stitch across the strap 2-inches down from the top edge to secure it to the front section. In the same manner stitch the remaining strap to the back section. The straps on the front section and back section should align.

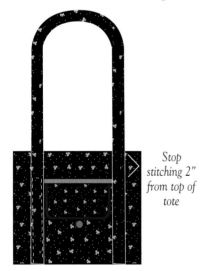

Step 12 Referring to the Fusible Fleece manufacturer's instructions, prepare the bottom section. Lay 11 x 15-inch fleece rectangle on ironing board (fusible side up). Position 11 x 15-inch **GOLD** rectangle on top of fleece (right side up). Cover with a press cloth; press to fuse. Machine quilt the layers together. <u>Trim bottom section to 9-1/2 x 13-1/2-inches.</u>

127

Step 13 With right sides together, sew the **GOLD** bottom rectangle to the prepared front using a 3/8-inch seam allowance. Sew the other side of the **GOLD** bottom to the prepared back. Press seam allowances toward **GOLD** bottom rectangle.

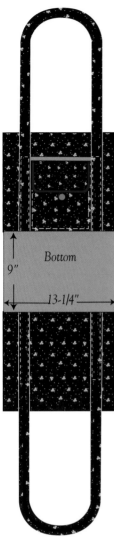

Step 14 With right sides together, sew the side seams of the bag using a 3/8-inch seam allowance. Refer to the diagram to make a flat bottom. With right sides together, match the side seams to the imaginary fold line on the bottom of the bag. Sew across both triangle tips approximately 1-3/4-inches from each point. **Do Not** trim off the triangle tips. Turn the bag right side out.

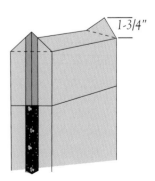

Step 15 With right sides together, fold a 13-1/2 x 14-1/2-inch **GOLD** rectangle in half so it measures 7-1/4 x 13-1/2-inches. Using a 1/4-inch seam allowance, stitch along the long edge. Turn the tube right side out; press. Edge-stitch along the top edge of the tube. Stitch 1/4-inch from the edge-stitching to help stabilize the top edge of the inner pocket. Make 2 inner pockets.

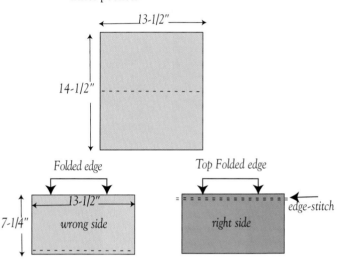

Step 16 To mark the right side of the 13-1/2 x 31-1/2-inch **BROWN DIAGONAL PRINT** lining rectangle with placement lines for the inner pocket, measure 13-1/2-inches in from both short edges of the lining, toward the center; draw a chalk line at each measurement. These are the placement lines for the <u>bottom</u> of the inner pockets.

Placement lines for pocket bottoms

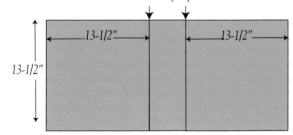

Step 17 Position a **GOLD** inner pocket along a placement line on the **BROWN DIAGONAL PRINT** lining. Baste side edges and edge-stitch in place along the bottom of the pocket. Stitch 1/4-inch from the edge-stitching to help stabilize the bottom edge. Stitch parallel lines through the inner pocket and lining for the desired pocket sections. Repeat to add the second inner pocket.

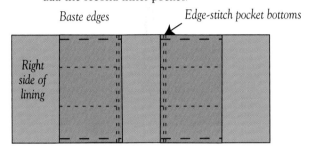

Baste edges   *Edge-stitch pocket bottoms*

Right side of lining

Step 18 With lining right sides together, sew the side seams using a 3/8-inch seam allowance. Refer to the Step 14 diagram and instructions to make a flat bottom in the lining.

Step 19 With <u>wrong sides together</u>, insert the lining into the tote. Baste the top edges of the tote and lining together with a scant 1/4-inch seam allowance.

Step 20 Prepare the 2-1/4 x 26-inch **RED** *bias* binding strip referring to **Binding** instructions on page 141. Aligning raw edges, position the binding strip on the top <u>outside edge</u> of the tote; stitch together with a 1/4-inch seam allowance. Turn the folded edge of the binding over the raw edges and to the inside of the bag. Hand sew the binding in place.

Step 21 Stitch across each strap to secure it to the top edge of the bag.

Step 22 To make the strap holder, fold the 4-1/2-inch **RED** square in half with right sides together; stitch. Turn right side out; press with seam in back. Fold one raw edge under 1/4-inch; press and stitch. Wrap the holder around both straps lapping the folded edge over the raw edges. Hand stitch the edges together to hold the two straps together.

fold   *seam*   *Fold and stitch*

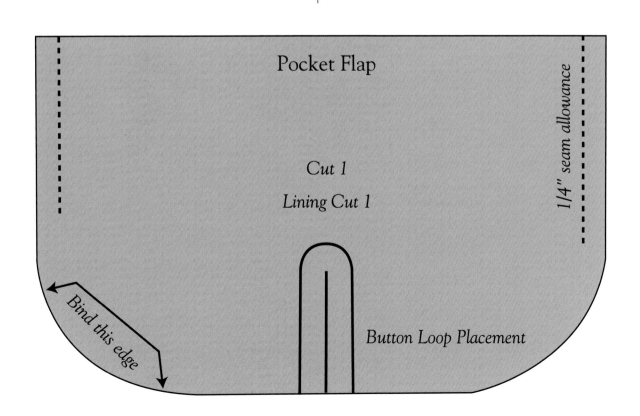

Pocket Flap

1/4" seam allowance

Cut 1

Lining Cut 1

Bind this edge

Button Loop Placement

General Instructions & Glossary

Getting Started

Yardage is based on 44-inch wide fabric. If your fabric is wider or narrower, it will affect the amount of necessary strips you need to cut in some patterns, and of course, it will affect the amount of fabric you have left over. Generally, Thimbleberries® patterns allow for a little extra fabric so you can confidently cut your pattern pieces with ease.

A rotary cutter, mat, and wide clear acrylic ruler with 1/8-inch markings are needed tools in attaining accuracy. A beginner needs good tools just as an experienced quiltmaker needs good equipment. A 24 x 36-inch cutting mat is a good size to own. It will easily accommodate the average quilt fabrics and will aid in accurate cutting. The acrylic ruler you purchase should be at least 6 x 24-inches and easy to read. Do not purchase a smaller ruler to save money. The large size will be invaluable to your quiltmaking success.

It is often recommended to prewash and press fabrics to test for colorfastness and possible shrinkage. If you choose to prewash, wash in cool water and dry in a cool to moderate dryer. Industry standards actually suggest that line drying is best. Shrinkage is generally very minimal and usually is not a concern. A good way to test your fabric for both shrinkage and colorfastness is to cut a 3-inch square of fabric. Soak the fabric in a white bowl filled with water. Squeeze the water out of the fabric and press it dry on a piece of muslin. If the fabric is going to release color, it will do so either in the water or when it is pressed dry. Remeasure the 3-inch fabric square to see if it has changed size considerably (more than 1/4-inch). If it has, wash, dry, and press the entire yardage. This little test could save you hours in prewashing and pressing.

Read instructions thoroughly before beginning a project. Each step will make more sense to you when you have a general overview of the whole process. Take one step at a time and follow the illustrations. They will often make more sense to you than the words. Take "baby steps" so you don't get overwhelmed by the entire process.

When working with flannel and other loosely woven fabrics, always prewash and dry. These fabrics almost always shrink more.

For piecing, place right sides of the fabric pieces together and use 1/4-inch seam allowances throughout the entire quilt unless otherwise specifically stated in the directions. An accurate seam allowance is the most important part of the quiltmaking process after accurately cutting. All the directions are based on accurate 1/4-inch seam allowances. It is very important to check your sewing machine to see what position your fabric should be to get accurate seams. To test, use a piece of 1/4-inch graph paper, stitch along the quarter inch line as if the paper were fabric. Make note of where the edge of the paper lines up with your presser foot or where it lines up on the throat plate of your machine. Many quilters place a piece of masking tape on the throat plate to help guide the edge of the fabric. Now test your seam allowance on fabric. Cut 2, 2-1/2-inch squares, place right sides together and stitch along one edge. Press seam allowances in one direction and measure. At this point the unit should measure 2-1/2 x 4-1/2-inches. If it does not, adjust your stitching guidelines and test again. Seam allowances are included in the cutting sizes given in this book.

Pressing is the third most important step in quiltmaking. As a general rule, you should never cross a stitched seam with another seam unless it has been pressed. Therefore, every time you stitch a seam, it needs to be pressed before adding another piece. Often, it will feel like you press as much as you sew, and often that is true. It is very important that you press and not iron the seams. Pressing is a firm, up-and-down motion that will flatten the seams but not distort the piecing. Ironing is a back-and-forth motion and will stretch and distort the small pieces. Most quilters use steam to help the pressing process. The moisture does help and will not distort the shapes as long as the pressing motion is used.

An old-fashioned rule is to press seam allowances in one direction, toward the darker fabric. Often, background fabrics are light in color and pressing

toward the darker fabric prevents the seam allowances from showing through to the right side. Pressing seam allowances in one direction is thought to create a stronger seam. Also, for ease in hand quilting, the quilting lines should fall on the side of the seam which is opposite the seam allowance. As you piece quilts, you will find these "rules" to be helpful but not neccesarily always appropriate. Sometimes seams need to be pressed in the opposite direction so the seams of different units will fit together more easily, which quilters refer to as seams "nesting" together. When sewing together two units with opposing seam allowances, use the tip of your seam ripper to gently guide the units under your presser foot. Sometimes it is necessary to re-press the seams to make the units fit together nicely. Always try to achieve the least bulk in one spot and accept that no matter which way you press, it may be a little tricky and it could be a little bulky.

Pressing Direction

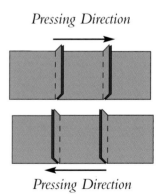

Pressing Direction

Squaring Up Blocks

To square up your blocks, first check the seam allowances. This is usually where the problem is, and it is always best to alter within the block rather than trim the outer edges. Next, make sure you have pressed accurately. Sometimes a block can become distorted by ironing instead of pressing.

To trim up block edges, use one of the many clear acrylic squares available on the market. Determine the center of the block; mark with a pin. Lay the square over the block and align as many perpendicular and horizontal lines as you can to the seams in your block. This will indicate where the block is off.

Do not trim all off on one side; this usually results in real distortion of the pieces in the block and the block design. Take a little fabric off all sides until the block is square. When assembling many blocks, it is necessary to make sure all are the same size.

Tools and Equipment

Making beautiful quilts does not require a large number of specialized tools or expensive equipment. My list of favorites is short and sweet and includes the things I use over and over again because they are always accurate and dependable.

I find a long acrylic ruler indispensable for accurate rotary cutting. The ones I like most are an Omnigrid® 6 x 24-inch grid acrylic ruler for cutting long strips and squaring up fabrics and quilt tops and a MasterPiece® 45-degree (8 x 24-inch) ruler for cutting 6- to 8-inch wide borders. I sometimes tape together two 6 x 24-inch acrylic rulers for cutting borders up to 12-inches wide.

A 15-inch Omnigrid® square acrylic ruler is great for squaring up individual blocks and corners of a quilt top, for cutting strips up to 15-inches wide or long, and for trimming side and corner triangles.

I think the markings on my 24 x 36-inch Olfa® rotary cutting mat stay visible longer than on other mats, and the lines are fine and accurate.

The largest size Olfa® rotary cutter cuts through many layers of fabric easily, and isn't cumbersome to use. The 2-1/2-inch blade slices through three layers of backing, batting, and a quilt top like butter.

An 8-inch pair of Gingher shears is great for cutting out appliqué templates and cutting fabric from a bolt or fabric scraps.

I keep a pair of 5-1/2-inch Gingher scissors by my sewing machine so it is handy for both machine work and handwork. This size is versatile and sharp enough to make large and small cuts equally well.

My Grabbit® magnetic pincushion has a surface that is large enough to hold lots of straight pins and a magnet strong enough to keep them securely in place.

Silk pins are long and thin, which means they won't leave large holes in your fabric. I like them because they increase accuracy in pinning pieces or blocks together. It is also easy to press over silk pins.

For pressing individual pieces, blocks, and quilt tops, I use an 18 x 48-inch sheet of plywood covered with several layers of cotton fiberfill and topped with a layer of muslin stapled to the back. The 48-inch length allows me to press an entire width of fabric at one time without the need to reposition it, and the square ends are better than tapered ends on an ironing board for pressing finished quilt tops.

Using Grain

The fabric you purchase still has selvage and before beginning to handle or cut your fabric, it's helpful to be able to recognize and understand its basic characteristics. Fabric is produced in the mill with identifiable grain or direction. These are: lengthwise, crosswise, and bias.

The lengthwise grain is the direction that fabric comes off the milling machine, and is parallel to the selvage. This grain of the fabric has the least stretch and the greatest strength.

The crosswise grain is the short distance that spans a bolt's 42-inch to 44-inch width. The crosswise grain, or width of grain, is between two sides called selvages. This grain of the fabric has medium stretch and medium strength.

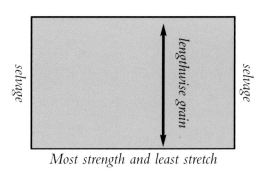
Most strength and least stretch

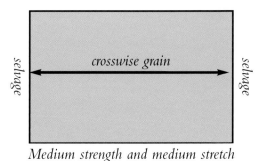
Medium strength and medium stretch

Avoiding Bias

The 45-degree angle on a piece of fabric is the bias and the direction with the most stretch. I suggest avoiding sewing on the bias until you're confident handling fabric. With practice and careful handling, bias edges can be sewn and are best for making curves.

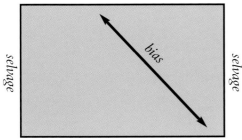

Least strength and most stretch

Rotary Cutting

SAFETY FIRST! The blades of a rotary cutter are very sharp and need to be for accurate cutting. Look at a variety of cutters to find one that feels good in your hand. All quality cutters have a safety mechanism to "close" the cutting blade when not in use. After each cut and before laying the rotary cutter down, close the blade. Soon this will become second nature to you and will prevent dangerous accidents. Always keep cutters out of the sight of children. Rotary cutters are very tempting to fiddle with when they are laying around. When your blade is dull or nicked, change it. Damaged blades do not cut accurately and require extra effort that can also result in slipping and injury. Also, always cut away from yourself for safety.

Squaring Off Fabric

Fold the fabric in half lengthwise matching the selvage edges.

Square off the ends of your fabric before measuring and cutting pieces. This means that the cut edge of the fabric must be exactly perpendicular to the folded edge which creates a 90-degree angle. Align the folded and selvage edges of the fabric with the lines on the cutting board, and place a ruled square on the fold. Place a 6 x 24-inch ruler against the side of the square to get a 90-degree angle. Hold the ruler in place, remove the square, and cut along the edge of the ruler. If you are left-handed, work from the other end of the fabric. Use the lines on your cutting board to help line up fabric, but not to measure and cut strips. Use a ruler for accurate cutting, always checking to make sure your fabric is lined up with horizontal and vertical lines on the ruler.

6 x 24" ruler

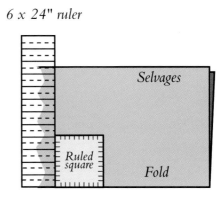

Cutting Strips

When cutting strips or rectangles, cut on the crosswise grain. Strips can then be cut into squares or smaller rectangles.

If your strips are not straight after cutting a few of them, refold the fabric, align the folded and selvage edges with the lines on the cutting board, and "square off" the edge again by trimming to straighten, and begin cutting.

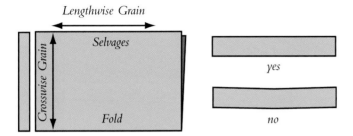

Lengthwise Grain

Crosswise Grain

Selvages

Fold

yes

no

Cutting Bias Strips

When cutting bias strips, trim your yardage on the crosswise grain so the edges are straight. With right sides facing up, fold the yardage on the diagonal. Fold the selvage edge (lengthwise grain) over to meet the cut edge (crosswise grain), forming a triangle. This diagonal fold is the true bias. Position the ruler to the desired strip width from the cut edge and cut one strip. Continue moving the ruler across the fabric cutting parallel strips in the desired widths.

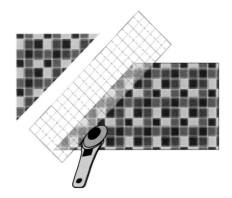

Trimming Side and Corner Triangles

In projects with side and corner triangles, the instructions have you cut side and corner triangles larger than needed. This will allow you to square up the quilt and eliminates the frustration of ending up with pre-cut side and corner triangles that don't match the size of your pieced blocks.

To cut triangles, first cut squares. The project directions will tell you what size to make the squares and whether to cut them in half to make two triangles or to cut them in quarters to make four triangles, as shown in the diagrams. This cutting method will give you side triangles that have the straight grain on the outside edges of the quilt. This is a very important part of quiltmaking that will help stabilize your quilt center.

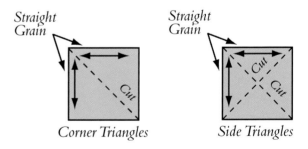

Straight Grain

Cut

Corner Triangles

Straight Grain

Cut

Cut

Side Triangles

Helpful Hints for Sewing with Flannel

Always prewash and machine dry flannel. This will prevent severe shrinkage after the quilt is made. Some flannels shrink more than others. For this reason, we have allowed approximately 1/4 yard extra for each fabric under the fabric requirements.

Treat the more heavily napped side of solid flannels as the right side of the fabric.

Because flannel stretches more than other cotton calicos and because the nap makes them thicker, the quilt design should be simple. Let the fabric and color make the design statement.

Consider combining regular cotton calicos with flannels. The different textures complement each other nicely.

Use a 10 to 12 stitches per inch setting on your machine. A 1/4-inch seam allowance is also recommended for flannel piecing.

When sewing triangle-pieced squares together, take extra care not to stretch the diagonal seam. Trim off the points from the seam allowances to eliminate bulk.

Press gently to prevent stretching pieces out of shape.

Check block measurements as you progress. "Square up" the blocks as needed. Flannel will shift and it is easy to end up with blocks that are misshapen. If you trim and measure as you go, you are more likely to have accurate blocks. If you notice a piece of flannel is stretching more than the others, place it on the bottom when stitching

on the machine. The natural action of the feed dogs will help prevent it from stretching.

Before stitching pieces, strips, or borders together, pin often to prevent fabric from stretching and moving. When stitching longer pieces together, divide the pieces into quarters and pin. Divide into even smaller sections to get more control.

Use a lightweight batting to prevent the quilt from becoming too heavy.

Cutting Triangles from Squares

Cutting accurate triangles can be intimidating for beginners, but a clear acrylic ruler, rotary cutter, and cutting mat are all that are needed to make perfect triangles. The cutting instructions often direct you to cut strips, then squares, and then triangles.

Sewing Layered Strips Together

When you are instructed to layer strips, right sides together, and sew, you need to take some precautions. Gently lay one strip on top of another, carefully lining up the raw edges. Pressing the strips together will hold them together nicely, and a few pins here and there will also help. Be careful not to stretch the strips as you sew them together.

Rod Casing or Sleeve to Hang Quilts

To hang wall quilts, attach a casing that is made of the same fabric as the quilt back. Attach this casing at the top of the quilt, just below the binding. Often, it is helpful to attach a second casing at the bottom of the quilt so you can insert a dowel into it which will help weight the quilt and make it hang free of ripples.

To make a rod casing or "sleeve," cut enough strips of fabric equal to the width of the quilt plus 2-inches for side hems. Generally, 6-inch wide strips will accommodate most rods. If you are using a rod with a larger diameter, increase the width of the strips.

Seam the strips together to get the length needed; press. Fold the strip in half lengthwise, wrong sides together. Stitch the long raw edges together with a 1/4-inch seam allowance. Center the seam on the backside of the sleeve; press. The raw edges of the seam will be concealed when the sleeve is stitched to the back of the quilt. Turn under both of the short raw edges; press and stitch to hem the ends. The final measurement should be about 1/2-inch from the quilt edges.

Pin the sleeve to the back of the quilt so the top edge of the sleeve is just below the binding. Hand stitch the top edge of the sleeve in place, then the bottom edge. Make sure to knot and secure your stitches at each end of the sleeve to make sure it will not pull away from the quilt with use. Slip the rod into the casing. If your wall quilt is not directional, making a sleeve for the bottom edge will allow you to turn your quilt end to end to relieve the stress at the top edge. You could also slip a dowel into the bottom sleeve to help anchor the lower edge of the wall quilt.

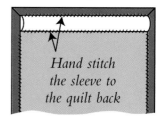

Hand stitch the sleeve to the quilt back

Hints and Helps for Pressing Strip Sets

When sewing strips of fabric together for strip sets, it is important to press the seam allowances nice and flat, usually to the darker fabric. Be careful not to stretch as you press, causing a "rainbow effect." This will affect the accuracy and shape of the pieces cut from the strip set. I like to press on the wrong side first and with the strips perpendicular to the ironing board. Then I flip the piece over and press on the right side to prevent little pleats from forming at the seams. Laying the strip set lengthwise on the ironing board seems to encourage the rainbow effect, as shown in the diagram.

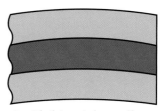

Avoid this rainbow effect

Borders

NOTE: Cut borders to the width called for. Always cut border strips a few inches longer than needed, just to be safe. Diagonally piece the border strips together as needed.

1. With pins, mark the center points along all 4 sides of the quilt. For the top and bottom borders, measure the quilt from left to right through the middle.

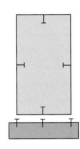

2. Measure and mark the border lengths and center points on the strips cut for the borders before sewing them on.

3. Pin the border strips to the quilt and stitch a 1/4-inch seam. Press the seam allowances toward the border. Trim off excess border lengths.

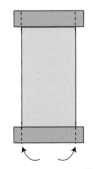

Trim away excess fabric

4. For the side borders, measure your quilt from top to bottom, including the borders just added, to determine the length of the side borders.

5. Measure and mark the side border lengths as you did for the top and bottom borders.

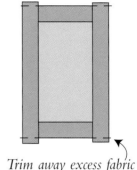

Trim away excess fabric

6. Pin and stitch the side border strips in place. Press and trim the border strips even with the borders just added.

7. If your quilt has multiple borders, measure, mark, and sew additional borders to the quilt in the same manner.

Decorative Stitches

Blanket Stitch

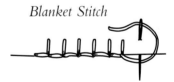

Outline/Stem Stitch

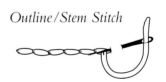

Straight Stitch

Choosing the Backing

The backing of any quilt is just as important to the overall design as the pieced patchwork top. Combine large-scale prints or piece coordinating fabrics together to create an interesting quilt back. Using large pieces of fabric (perhaps three different prints that are the same length as the quilt) or a large piece of fabric that is bordered by compatible prints, keeps the number of seams to a minimum, which speeds up the process. The new 108-inch wide fabric sold on the bolt eliminates the need for seaming entirely. Carefully selected fabrics for a well-constructed backing not only complement a finished quilt, but make it more useful as a reversible accent.

Crib— 45 x 60-inches

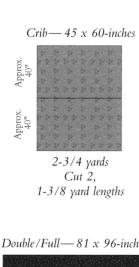

Approx. 40"

Approx. 40"

2-3/4 yards
Cut 2,
1-3/8 yard lengths

Twin—72 x 90-inches

Approx. 40"   Approx. 40"
5-1/3 yards
Cut 2, 2-2/3 yard lengths

Double/Full— 81 x 96-inches

Approx. 40"

Approx. 40"

Approx. 40"

7-1/8 yards
Cut 3, 2-3/8 yard lengths

Queen—90 x 108-inches

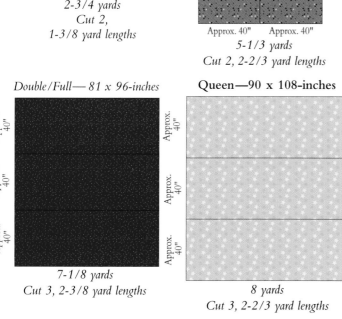

Approx. 40"

Approx. 40"

Approx. 40"

8 yards
Cut 3, 2-2/3 yard lengths

Finishing the Quilt

1. Remove the selvages from the backing fabric. Sew the long edges together and press. Trim the backing and batting so they are 4-inches to 6-inches larger than the quilt top.

2. Mark the quilt top for quilting. Layer the backing, batting, and quilt top. Baste the 3 layers together and quilt.

3. When quilting is complete, remove basting. Hand baste all 3 layers together a scant 1/4-inch from the edge. This hand basting keeps the layers from shifting and prevents puckers from forming when adding the binding. Trim excess batting and backing fabric even with the edge of the quilt top. Add the binding as shown below.

Binding and Diagonal Piecing

1. Diagonally piece the binding strips. Fold the strip in half lengthwise, wrong sides together, and press.

Diagonal Piecing

Stitch diagonally   *Trim to 1/4-inch seam allowance*   *Press seam open*

2. Unfold and trim one end at a 45-degree angle. Turn under the edge 3/8-inch and press. Refold the strip.

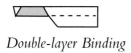

Double-layer Binding

3. With raw edges of the binding and quilt top even, stitch with a 3/8-inch seam allowance, starting 2-inches from the angled end.

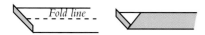

4. Miter the binding at the corners. As you approach a corner of the quilt, stop sewing 3/8-inch from the corner of the quilt.

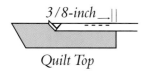

Quilt Top

5. Clip the threads and remove the quilt from under the presser foot. Flip the binding strip up and away from the quilt, then fold the binding down even with the raw edge of the quilt. Begin sewing at the upper edge. Miter all 4 corners in this manner.

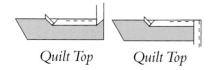

Quilt Top   *Quilt Top*

6. Trim the end of the binding so it can be tucked inside of the beginning binding about 1/2-inch. Finish stitching the seam.

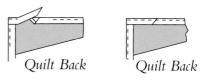

Quilt Back   *Quilt Back*

7. Turn the folded edge of the binding over the raw edges and to the back of the quilt so that the stitching line does not show. Hand sew the binding in place, folding in the mitered corners as you stitch.

Quilt Back   *Quilt Back*   *Quilt Back*

Glossary

Appliqué The sewing technique for attaching pieces (appliqués) of fabric onto a background fabric. Appliqués may be stitched to the background by hand, using a blind stitch, or by machine, using a satin stitch or a blind hemstitch.

Backing The bottom layer of a quilt consisting of one whole piece of fabric or several fabrics joined together.

Basting The technique for joining layers of fabric or the layers of a quilt with safety pins (pin basting) or large stitches (hand basting). The pinning or stitching is temporary and is removed after permanent stitching.

Batting A layer of filler placed between two pieces of fabric to form a quilt. Its thickness and fiber content varies.

Bias The grain of woven fabric that is at a 45-degree angle to the selvages. The bias grain has more stretch and is less stable than the crosswise or lengthwise grain.

Bias strips Strips of fabric cut on the bias and joined to make one continuous strip for binding that can easily be positioned around curved edges.

Binding The strip of fabric used to cover the outside edges—top, batting and backing—of a quilt.

Block A basic unit, usually square and often repeated, of a quilt top.

Borders The framing on a quilt that serves to visually hold in the design and give the eye a stopping point.

Crosscutting Cutting fabric strips into smaller units, such as squares or rectangles.

Crosswise grain The threads running perpendicular to the selvage across the width of a woven fabric.

Cutting mat Surface used for rotary cutting that protects the tabletop and keeps the fabric from shifting while cutting. Often mats are labeled as self-healing, meaning the blade does not leave slash marks or grooves in the surface even after repeated use.

Double-fold binding Binding made from a fabric strip that is folded in half before being attached to the quilt. Also, referred to as French-fold binding.

Finished size The measurement of a completed block or quilt.

Free-motion or machine quilting A process of quilting done with the feed dogs disengaged and using a darning presser foot so the quilt can be moved freely on the machine bed in any direction.

Grain The direction of woven fabric. The crosswise grain is from selvage to selvage. The lengthwise grain runs parallel to the selvage and is stronger. The bias grain is at a 45-degree angle and has the greatest amount of stretch.

Hand quilting Series of running stitches made through all layers of a quilt with needle and thread.

Hanging sleeve Tube of fabric that is attached to the quilt back. A wooden dowel is inserted through the fabric tube to hang the quilt. It is also called a rod pocket and used with a board or rod as a support to hang a quilt on the wall.

Inner border A strip of fabric, usually more narrow than the outer border, that frames the quilt center.

Layering Placing the quilt top, batting, and quilt backing on top of each other in layers.

Lengthwise grain The threads running parallel to the selvage in a woven fabric.

Longarm quilting A quilting machine used by professional quilters in which the quilt is held taut on a frame that allows the quilter to work on a large portion of the quilt at a time. The machine head moves freely, allowing the operator to use free-motion to quilt in all directions.

Machine quilting Series of stitches made through all layers of a quilt sandwich with a sewing machine.

Marking tools A variety of pens, pencils, and chalks that can be used to mark fabric pieces or a quilt top.

Mitered seam A 45-degree angle seam.

Outer border A strip of fabric that is joined to the edges of the quilt top to finish or frame it.

Pieced border Blocks or pieced units sewn together to make a single border unit that is then sewn to the quilt center.

Piecing The process of sewing pieces of fabric together.

Pressing Using an iron with an up and down motion to set stitches and flatten a seam allowance, rather than sliding it across the fabric.

Quilt center The quilt top before borders are added.

Quilt top Top layer of a quilt usually consisting of pieced blocks.

Quilting The small running stitches made through the layers of a quilt (quilt top, batting and backing) to form decorative patterns on the surface of the quilt and hold the layers together.

Quilting stencils Quilting patterns with open areas through which a design is transferred onto a quilt top. May be purchased or made from sturdy, reusable template plastic.

Rotary cutter Tool with a sharp, round blade attached to a handle that is used to cut fabric. The blade is available in different diameters.

Rotary cutting The process of cutting fabric into strips and pieces using a revolving blade rotary cutter, a thick, clear acrylic ruler, and a special cutting mat.

Running stitches A series of in-and-out stitches used in hand quilting.

Seam allowance The 1/4-inch margin of fabric between the stitched seam and the raw edge.

Selvage The lengthwise finished edge on each side of the fabric.

Slipstitch A hand stitch used for finishing such as sewing binding to a quilt where the thread is hidden by slipping the needle between a fold of fabric and tacking down with small stitches.

Squaring up or straightening fabric The process of trimming the raw edge of the fabric so it creates a 90-degree angle with the folded edge of the fabric. Squaring up is also a term used when trimming a quilt block.

Strip sets Two or more strips of fabric, cut and sewn together along the length of the strips.

Triangle-pieced square The square unit created when two 90-degree triangles are sewn together on the diagonal.

Unfinished size The measurement of a block before the 1/4-inch seam allowance is sewn or the quilt is quilted and bound.